Counselling in Schools

don't take sides — need
to even with all groups (child,
family, school)
ask questions
do not make assumptions

Genogram

Endorsements for Counselling in Schools

Counselling in Schools

Robert Bor, Jo Ebner-Landy,
Sheila Gill and Chris Brace

SAGE Publications
London • Thousand Oaks • New Delhi

First published 2002

 SAGE Publications Ltd
6 Bonhill Street
London EC2A 4PU

SAGE Publications Inc
2455 Teller Road
Thousand Oaks, California 91320

SAGE Publications India Pvt Ltd
32, M-Block Market
Greater Kailash - I
New Delhi 110 048

British Library Cataloguing in Publication data

A catalogue record for this book is available from
the British Library.

ISBN 0 7619 7275 7
ISBN 0 7619 7276 5 (pbk)

Library of Congress Control Number available

Typeset by SIVA Math Setters, Chennai, India
Printed in Great Britain by Biddles Ltd, Guildford, Surrey

In loving memory of Katherine.

To all the pupils, families and colleagues at schools with whom we have had the privilege to work.

Contents

About the Authors

Robert Bor is Professor of Psychology at London Guildhall University and also works as a counsellor at a school in London. He is a Chartered Clinical, Counselling and Health Psychologist and a UKCP Registered Family Therapist. He received specialist training in family therapy at the Tavistock Clinic, London and is a member of the Tavistock Society of Psychotherapists. He is extensively involved in counsellor training and research. He has published numerous books and papers on counselling. He is a member of the Institute of Family Therapy, London, American Family Therapy Academy, American Psychological Association, and American Association for Marital and Family Therapy. He is also in private practice as a psychologist. He also has an interest in aviation psychology and is a qualified pilot. Robert Bor is a Churchill Fellow.

Jo Ebner-Landy trained as a primary school teacher at Homerton College, Cambridge University and completed her Masters of Arts degree at the Institute of Education, London. She trained in Counselling at City University, London and in family therapy at the Institute of Family Therapy, London. She is an experienced school counsellor and teacher at both primary and secondary levels; she is currently teaching in a London primary school and is a school counsellor and a consultant on counselling matters in two schools. She has recently commenced work on a Doctorate.

Sheila Gill is a BACP Accredited Counsellor, UKRC Registered Independent Counsellor and an accredited Member of Counsellors in Primary Care. She is an experienced systemic therapist and trainer. She holds a Postgraduate Diploma in Counselling in Primary Care from City University and a Certificate in Systemic Therapy from Kensington Consultation Centre. She works as a counsellor in the London School of Economics and in a general practice in North London. Her particular interest is in applying systemic and constructionist ideas to working with individuals, couples and families and within organisations.

Chris Brace graduated from the University of York in 1997 with an Honours degree in Psychology. He is currently undertaking postgraduate study at Goldsmith's College, London. He has worked at London Guildhall University for the last 18 months and is extensively involved in the management of trainee counselling psychologists.

Acknowledgements

We gratefully acknowledge the guidance and support of a number of colleagues.

Mr R. S. Baldock, the Highmaster of St Paul's School, London, read early drafts of the book and his feedback and comments are very much appreciated.

The teachers and staff at our respective schools have helped to raise the awareness and importance of attending to the personal and psychological needs of pupils.

Our publisher, Alison Poyner of Sage Publications, was enthusiastic about the book from the start and provided every support along the road to publication. Rachel Burrows, the Production Editor, helped us with the revisions to the manuscript.

Our own families have provided us with the time and space to write this book.

Perhaps the greatest acknowledgement must go to those children, families and colleagues who have shared with us their personal concerns and experiences in counselling and consultation sessions. We are enormously grateful to everyone who has helped to shape our own ideas about counselling.

Appendices

Appendix A, 'Confidentiality: Counselling and the Law', Appendix B, 'Confidentiality Guidelines for College Counsellors in Further Education and Sixth Form Colleges' and Appendix F, 'Access to Records of Counselling and Psychotherapy' are reproduced with the kind permission of the British Association for Counselling and Psychotherapy, the copyright holder.

1 Introduction

The field of counselling and psychotherapy in schools

Over the last few years there has been a huge growth of interest in the fields of counselling and psychotherapy. This has manifested itself in a number of areas: in health care, in the family, in the workplace and, of course, in schools. The development of a separate specialty of counselling in schools has in part resulted from the decline of the traditional pastoral roles that teachers used to take on. They often find little time to undertake the extracurricular activities which in many countries were the normal expectation for all teachers. Indeed, teachers have recently been constrained by the National Curriculum, Standard Assessment Tasks (SATs) and the general and very real pressures of work. Moreover, students have become more aware of their 'rights' and are often the ones asking for counselling support to help them face the emotional hazards of growing up. The parents of young adults and children are keen to have a supportive adult in school with whom their children can share problems; often it is they who have been instrumental in asking a headteacher and school governors to employ a school counsellor. The requirements of the Children Act 1989 for pastoral provision in schools has encouraged some schools to set up a formalised counselling service. Headteachers of schools also recognise that the skills of psychotherapists and counsellors can be fruitfully employed in dealing with the tremendous range of problems that pupils present with.

Books about child and adolescent psychopathology abound. However, there are far fewer books on counselling and psychotherapy in schools. The school is a more recent context for the provision of psychological treatment of young people and until ten years ago most mental problems were referred to specialists outside the school setting. The impetus for recent changes to this and for the development of school-based counselling has a number of causes.

1 Everyday life can be challenging and stressful for even the most resilient of children. Competitiveness, bullying, social exclusion, racism, family crises, sibling rivalry, scholastic underachievement, abuse, homophobia, peer pressure and substance misuse are but a few of the problems brought by children to the average school counsellor's office.
2 Like home, schools are considered a primary and essential context for supporting, nurturing and facilitating educational, moral and social development in young people.
3 There is increasing awareness of the role that schools play in identifying, managing and preventing mental health problems in young people.

4   There is a shortage of specialist educational psychologists, many of whom are required to work with more exceptional or needy children. Common personal, emotional and social problems may go unnoticed in average children by busy teachers.

5   Early identification of psychological problems (be they transient or more entrenched) can prevent major and more permanent behavioural problems in children. The government requires schools to be inclusive institutions. Children attend from a wide range of backgrounds and abilities. 'Ecological assessments' of youngsters help to identify unique and specific problems that may require attention by the school (rather than one that views them as deficient and inseparably different) and counsellors have a role to play in these assessments.

6   Rare but headline-catching atrocities committed by some children (e.g. the murders at Columbine and Santana high schools in the USA and of Damilola Taylor in the UK) have been the impetus behind efforts to understand and prevent violence among youth. Problems such as suicide and homicide may be avoidable in some cases and counsellors may have a role in preventing tragedies of these kinds. Some atrocities are witnessed by school children, such as those in Brooklyn, NY who saw the World Trade Centre being hit by hijacked aircraft in 2001. Such horrific incidents may have serious psychological consequences.

7   Counselling as a profession is now better managed and regulated and there is an improved understanding of the benefits and limits of counselling practice.

8   Some counsellors are more willing to work collaboratively with other colleagues in school settings as members of the staff team, thereby removing some of the mystique and scepticism previously associated with their practice.

9   Schools are organisations and counsellors who have an understanding of group and organisational processes have the potential to contribute to the development of that organisation through systems-oriented interventions.

Brief history of counselling in schools

In order to understand counselling in schools, we first need to examine something of its history and development. Counselling in schools is by no means a new phenomenon, although the media would often like to present it as such. As far back as 1913, the London County Council appointed its first child psychologist to examine 'dull, backward and feeble minded children and to give guidance to teachers and parents on the treatment and education of children attending ordinary schools' (cited by Milner, 1974).

School counselling is well established in the USA and dates back to 1898 where the Central School in Detroit had a school counsellor. However, it was not until the 1960s that school counselling began to develop in the UK. The 1963 Newsom Report focused on the needs of pupils who were failing to reach their true potential in school and recommended that school counsellors should be employed. As a result of these recommendations, some counselling courses were set up in universities such as Reading and Keele for the training of school counsellors. These courses were only available to trained teachers who had at least five years' teaching experience. By the 1970s there were several hundred school counsellors in England and Wales and nine full-time courses at various universities throughout the country. In 1973 there were 18 courses such as Guidance and Counselling in Education at Reading or the Full-time Diploma courses in School Counselling at Swansea and North East London Polytechnic. Some local education authorities also developed counselling services in their schools. The Association of School Counselling was set up to provide a professional organisation for anyone concerned with the counselling of students and young people.

However, it seems that the enthusiasm for these university courses was short lived. In the absence of government backing, a feeling emerged that school counsellors were an unnecessary extravagance in schools (Jones, 1970). By the 1970s school counselling was provided in an ad hoc sort of way. In the 1980s there was a shift in emphasis on counselling in schools. The local education authorities felt that it was the teachers who needed to be taking the responsibility for pastoral care and that counselling should be integrated into their teaching practice and be part of their role as teachers (Hamblin, 1974). Some schools continued to employ counsellors, whereas others trained their teaching staff to have a dual role. There were few guidelines for practice, just as there are few now. Counsellors were free to develop counselling services leading to different roles, relationships and styles of practice. Currently there are still a few courses specifically geared towards training counsellors to work in schools, although there is a range of general counselling and therapy courses on offer, as well as the educational therapy training.

In recent years school counselling has again begun to take a more prominent role in schools. Teachers are under huge pressures to teach, keep detailed records on their pupils and fulfil all the criteria of the National Curriculum. As a result of this pressure, teachers can often find it difficult to take on the added pastoral role. Some schools have thus begun to realise the benefits of employing a counsellor. The usefulness is increasingly recognised of having someone on site who is available to all the pupils, not only to meet their educational needs, but also to meet the emotional and psychological needs of pupils, thereby contributing to the emotional well-being of the whole school.

Conceptual issues

There is as yet no single guideline or template for how a school-based counselling service should be set up and operated. This is largely left to the individual institution and counsellor to conceive and develop. Understandably, this has resulted in a fair amount of diversity in practice. However, there is a common link in some school-based counselling practices which reflects a more traditional and frequently inflexible approach to clinical work. The approach is summarised in Box 1.1.

Box 1.1

Traditional ethos of counsellors working in schools

- The presenting problem is viewed as residing within the individual child.
- The individual child is almost exclusively the focus or target of intervention.
- The emphasis in counselling sessions tends to be on the child's pathology and dysfunction.
- The counsellor operates separately from other staff at school and professional boundaries are sometimes rigidly preserved.
- The inclusion of other family members (especially parents) into sessions is avoided and sometimes strenuously resisted.
- Counselling may be explorative or long term and there may be no requirement in terms of a model of counselling and practice to intervene directly, explicitly and in a time-conscious way where problems present.

Many readers might not readily identify any or all of these underpinnings to practice. However, they are included to remind readers of the more traditional approaches and styles of practice still commonly associated with counselling young people. It is an unfortunate fact that the dominant approach to counselling children in schools is still characterised by many of the practices listed in the box. Contemporary and parsimonious counselling approaches have paved the way for new possibilities in school-based counselling. The authors have developed their practice in different school settings in London. We have sought to identify and describe in this book the common threads of practice and theoretical underpinnings that inform our counselling work and are consistent with an emerging trend towards systemic and time-sensitive consultations with children, their families and the school (see also Davis and Osborne, 2000; Dowling and Osborne, 1994). A summary of these ideas and practices is presented in Box 1.2.

Box 1.2

Ethos of systemic counsellors working in schools

- The school counsellor is a part of a wider organisational context and is therefore attuned to focusing on systems and interrelatedness in this setting.
- While an individual child might initially present with a problem, this problem (and hence its onset, maintenance and resolution) may involve others connected with the child (e.g. family, friends and peers, teachers, etc.). To this end, every clinical problem engenders a whole ecology of relationships which needs to be addressed. (Note: this is not to imply that all of these 'players' should be required to participate in counselling sessions, but at the very least their influence and impact on the child and problem should be addressed with the child.)

- Confining practice to the counselling room may be limiting and ultimately self-defeating. The counsellor should also be available to consult other staff about problems they are required to manage in the classroom and elsewhere at school. Opportunities for participation and involvement in the everyday life of the school can be exploited without compromising the integrity of the counsellor among the pupils.
- Awareness of professional boundaries and the requirement for confidentiality does not preclude collaboration with teachers and other professionals at school. Indeed, collaboration is seen to promote and enhance effective and ethical client practice.
- Counsellors work collaboratively with their clients. They shun the concept that 'the adult (or counsellor) knows best' in all situations. They also avoid subscribing to the concept that 'deep and dark secrets about the child are revealed through counselling'. The counsellor elicits the child's coping resources and ideas wherever possible to solve problems. A normative base for clinical practice ('You must/should/ ought to...') which is prescriptive and value laden is avoided by the counsellor, except where there is the danger of harm to the child. The potential for biases and normative views inadvertently to find their way into the counsellor's repertoire are addressed in their regular supervision sessions.
- The counsellor has a genuine empathy with the client and makes no assumptions about the nature of the problem or its effect on the child. The counsellor devotes copious amounts of time in counselling sessions to trying to understand and clearly define the problem and learn about the child's experiences of having to cope with it.
- A clearly espoused theoretical approach is imperative for good practice. The essentials of the approach should be evident and teachable to other professionals at school, though much of the detail of practice need not. To this end, school counsellors should make their practice transparent and ensure that there is a firm basis of evidence for their clinical work.
- Counselling should be purposeful and, wherever appropriate, brief unless there is an explicit understanding and agreement that an explorative and open-ended arrangement is more suited to dealing with the problem.
- Solution-focused or brief counselling is neither shallow nor ineffective. All the available evidence suggests that these approaches can be highly effective and require a concerted effort in sessions to clearly define the problem and map progress towards its resolution (Berg and Miller, 1992; Budman and Gurman, 1992).
- Problems are usually conveyed through language and therefore counselling sessions are likely to be transacted as conversations between child and counsellor. At times, however, other ways of relating will take precedence in a child-oriented counselling service. With younger children the technique of play therapy can be usefully employed. Non-verbal communication, silences, play and humour are all possible. The professional and confident counsellor is responsive to the child's needs.
- The counsellor always believes that some change is possible, even with the most challenging of problems. Some of these changes,

however, can take place outside counselling sessions. Children have 'real' lives outside counselling sessions! They also have friends and family members from whom they can solicit support.

- Pathologising labels and undue focus on dysfunction tend to constrain the counsellor and impede the therapeutic relationship. On the other hand, the school counsellor requires a comprehensive understanding of child and adolescent development, psychopathology and the nomenclature for diagnostic categories, as these are useful when consulting other professionals about a case. Counsellors need, however, to be alert to the danger that pathologising labels may lead the counsellor down a path of constraint and impossibility. The counsellor's capacity for receptive openness and creativity is inversely proportional to the amount of pathologising terms and psychobabble uttered.

Aims of the book

In an effort to provide counsellors, headteachers, teachers, pastoral caregivers, school and college nurses and doctors, family therapists and all other allied professionals with a contemporary guide, the authors describe a theoretical base and examples of practice for counselling in secondary schools. The range of chapters covered will:

- examine the need for a school-based counselling service and discuss the range of possible psychological problems with which pupils may present;
- describe the role of the school counsellor in relation to working with pupils, and discuss how to set up consultation with parents and teachers;
- present a systemic and solution-focused framework for counselling that takes into account not only the individual, but also his or her family and the school context in which counselling takes place;
- examine through case examples, both short and long, some of the specific problems a school counsellor may have to face and demonstrate solutions using brief, solution-focused counselling in school settings;
- address practical and legal issues, (e.g. child protection, abuse, confidentiality;) and explore the issues of counsellor competence, defining boundaries and referring cases on to other agencies;
- consider the counsellor's relationship with others, such as the headteacher and pastoral staff, as well as discussing the role of the supervisor;
- examine the tasks and practical skills that are required to set up and evaluate a counselling service;
- describe how the counsellor works with trauma, such as the death of a pupil and look at how to set up a disaster recovery plan;
- give examples of policies and guidelines (e.g. anti-bullying policy; BACP Code of Ethics) that may be used in schools and school-based counselling services.

We have specifically avoided including a chapter on adolescent problems because the teacher will find more detailed information on these in other specialist books (e.g. Copley and Forryan, 1997; Daws and Boston, 1981; Geldard, and Geldard, 1999a, 1999b; Lanyado and Horne, 1999; Newcombe, 1996). Instead, we have endeavoured to illustrate the possible range of presenting problems and issues through vignettes and case studies. Some of these include conflict with parents, sibling rivalry, anxiety, cultural issues, bullying, physical illness, loss, sexuality and abuse, among others. Irrespective of the nature of the presenting problem, and the counsellor's perceived competence for treating such a problem, there is a host of generic tasks and skills that can be brought to bear in any client encounter. These primarily concern problem exploration and definition, leading to problem management. Detailed knowledge and experience of treating every conceivable psychological problem is not required by counsellors these days. Of far greater relevance is an ability to relate to a troubled child or teenager, his parents and school teachers, and having the confidence and resources to clearly define the problem.

All of the case examples described in this book come from real cases seen by the authors. However, the identifying details have been changed in order to preserve confidentiality.

Chapters 2 and 3 present an overview of the key conceptual issues in systemic and solution-focused counselling in schools. In Chapters 4 and 5 we describe the practice of counselling and list the skills necessary to work with children, families and other professional colleagues. A case example comprises Chapter 6 in order to illustrate further the application of some of the ideas already presented. Chapter 7 addresses legal and confidentiality issues, while Chapter 8 covers the school's response to traumatic incidents and the counsellor's role in this. The remaining chapters address organisational and practical details such as setting up a school counselling service (Chapter 9), and evaluating counselling (Chapter 10). The Appendices contain: (a) the BACP Confidentiality Guidelines; (b) those pertaining to further education and sixth form colleges; (c) an extract from the Guidelines for University and College Counselling Services; (d) bullying and harassment: policy and guidelines; (e) a list of basic genogram symbols; (f) BACP information sheet on Access to Records of Counselling and Psychotherapy.

The book mainly addresses counselling in secondary schools, although the ideas can readily be adapted for use in sixth form colleges, primary schools, further education colleges and other educational settings.

Some readers may prefer greater clarity from the authors about the terms 'client', 'adolescent', 'child', 'counselling', 'psychotherapy' and the personal pronouns used for counsellor and clients. We specifically do not intend to antag-onise and we offer a brief explanation. First, this book is written with secondary school counsellors in mind. Obviously some of the ideas can be adapted for use in primary schools, colleges or universities. The terms 'client', 'adolescent', 'child', and 'pupil' are therefore used interchangeably. Second, some counsellors and psychotherapists hold (or are taught to hold) firm views that the terms 'coun-selling' and 'psychotherapy' are not interchangeable and they may be disturbed by our apparent lack of regard for clarity. However, for ease and simplicity, we mostly use the terms 'counsellor' and 'counselling' rather than 'psychotherapist' and 'psychotherapy' with the understanding that, irrespective of core training received, all of us are striving to work therapeutically. Third, as practitioners, we are extremely sensitive to the language we use and as far as possible avoid sexist or stereotypical terms. However, for clarity of style, we mostly refer to the counsellor as 'she' and the client as 'he'. This does not reflect any bias on the part of the authors.

Finally, this book is designed to serve as a guide to practice. The ideas are in no way intended to be prescriptive. We recognise that each school and counselling service will require unique and specific approaches. These may change over time as new and unanticipated problems are encountered, staff change and different personalities are involved in these services, laws change pertaining to child care, different approaches to treatment are documented and taught, and the practice of counselling evolves. Central to working professionally as a counsellor is accepting that change is inevitable in one's own context and practice. One task for the counsellor is therefore to manage change within a wide range of systems and simultaneously to create a sense of stability. Anyone who works with children or in a thriving organisation is confronted with a similar challenge. We hope that some of the ideas described in this book illustrate ways of addressing this challenge.

2 Setting the Scene

An Overview of Working as a Counsellor with Young Children

Counselling can help young people to cope with and adjust to new and unwelcome circumstances. It can also help other family members to adapt to these changes. However, the notion of 'needing counselling' can inadvertently create a problem and undermine an individual's ability to cope and adapt. Some examples of questions we have been asked by counsellors will help to open up some of these issues for further scrutiny:

- Where does a counsellor fit into the school structure?
- What is the role and task of the counsellor within the school setting?
- Does the counsellor need to have detailed knowledge about a child's life in order to counsel him about it?
- How do confidentiality rules apply in school settings?
- How can you work with a child who has been referred for counselling but does not want it?
- How do you work with family members?

This book will address some of these questions by providing the reader with the theory and skills necessary to counsel children effectively within the boundaries of a school setting. It will do this in reference to the systems approach which takes into account the interrelationship of the child, the family and the school, and how the actions and attitudes of each affects the other.

Some people remember their schooldays as having been the best days of their lives, but others regard them as having been a painful experience. By the time children reach 16 years of age, they will have been at school for 11 years – a substantial part of their lives. During this time they will have had to face the myriad problems of growing up; how to forge and sustain relationships with others; how to study; how to respect figureheads; how societal hierarchy works; how to deal with peer pressure; how to develop a sense of self; how to time manage; how to resolve conflict. On top of these, there is the emergence of puberty and the accompanying discovery of sexuality. The emphasis is on constant adaptation and coping with changes both inside and outside the concept of 'self'. For many, this will be a fantastic voyage ending in the discovery of a new world, but for others the path will be beset with perils that can only be overcome with a sympathetic ear and gentle guidance in the right direction. Working therapeutically with children and adolescents sometimes requires different ideas and skills of the counsellor to working with adults.

Working with adolescents

This book focuses on the necessary skills and concepts to practise systemic, solution-focused counselling in a school counselling context. The emphasis is on working with pupils in secondary schools, although the ideas can be adapted for use when working with younger pupils. No book of this kind would be complete without some guidelines for working with children and adolescents, and the following section aims to provide these. Readers who feel that they require in-depth knowledge or a refresher of child development and child and adolescent psychopathology are encouraged to consult other textbooks such as: *Attachment Behaviour and the Schoolchild: An Introduction to Educational Therapy* (Barrett and Trevitt, 1991); *Therapeutic Work with Young People* (Copley and Forryan, 1997); *The Child Psychotherapist and Problems of Young People* (Daws and Boston, 1981); *The Handbook of Child and Adolescent Psychotherapy* (Lanyado and Horne, 1999); *Child Development* (Newcombe, 1996).

Adolescence is a time of physiological, cognitive and psychological changes. Adolescents need time to understand and integrate all the enormous changes taking place in the period between childhood and adulthood. In some areas they may be able to make decisions like an adult, but in others they may feel unsure and childlike. For the adolescent poised between childhood and adulthood, risk taking and experimentation are normal activities.

Parents must strike a balance between promoting independence and setting boundaries for their adolescent children. While wishing to escape the limits of authority in order to achieve freedom, the adolescent, through fear of the unknown, may wish for greater boundary setting and resistance from parents. Some parents may respond by becoming overprotective, while others may be tempted to allow their child greater freedom.

Peer pressure to have a sexual relationship and talk about it in a competitive atmosphere, experiment with alcohol, drugs and other potentially risky activities places great stress on all adolescents. The counselling of adolescents differs in some ways from counselling adults. There are particular aspects of counselling which are unique to this age group and may be challenging for the counsellor. Adolescents require tact and sensitivity in order to engage their attention sufficiently to enlist their co-operation. Counsellors must make clear statements, using language understood by the adolescent. The counsellor should not make assumptions about how much has been understood in the session. She should ask questions to check the extent of the adolescent's knowledge and reinforce the information. Counsellors may find themselves facilitating conversations between adolescents and their parents or guardians. Parents may wish to have some time to discuss their concerns apart from the family interview, which includes the adolescent. Decisions about this should be made after open discussion to avoid suggesting that the counsellor might be viewed as having an alliance with either parents or adolescent.

Guidelines for the counsellor

Rapport must be established so as to enable the adolescent to discuss what may seem to be difficult topics. Brief conversations, with elements of surprise and some humour, may engage the adolescent more easily than long discussions, which often result in a loss of concentration.

Consider how the referral may affect counselling. Although the adolescent will probably have been referred to the counsellor by his teacher, tutor, parents or other figures in authority, he is likely to be far less reluctant if he has asked for help himself. The adolescent will quite possibly demonstrate feelings of resistance, scepticism and a distrust of counselling. These feelings are appropriate to the situation. He may indicate what he feels by coming late or missing appointments, not taking advice from the counsellor, or through non-verbal behaviours such as chewing gum, not talking or putting his feet on office furniture. The counsellor will be an unwelcome figure for most adolescents. It would probably be strange if this were not the view of these young clients. The counsellor must therefore accept that in some cases she is working with a 'resistant' client.

To avoid an argument, the counsellor might attempt to deal with reluctance by sharing the adolescent's scepticism about counselling, if this becomes an issue, and confirming his views. As in the adolescent's relationships with his parents, the counsellor needs to balance this approach with a firmness which conveys boundaries and gives him something to 'push' against. The alternative, in some cases, is for the counsellor to battle on, trying to convince the adolescent of her view, incurring a major act of defiance. The adolescent may opt out of sessions, ending any further influence over him.

One of the aims of counselling an adolescent is to normalise his situation for him, as much as possible under the circumstances, without denying the reality of his problem. On the one hand, the counsellor can help him to grow and develop as a person, to experiment, to take some risks, to be rebellious and to have hopes and dreams for his future. On the other hand, the counsellor has to try to help him not to endanger himself or others. She should help the adolescent to acquire a clearer and acceptable view of his problem. Harm minimisation, to himself and others, is a guiding theme for the counsellor. However, it is improbable and inappropriate that the counsellor will be able to eliminate every risk situation in the adolescent's life.

Some adolescents will view the counsellor as intrusive and meddlesome. We try to convey to our clients that we *cannot instruct* them or make them do anything they do not want to do. As counsellors, we are not agents of social control. Instead, we try to enhance the responsibility of the client. There are a number of practical steps that the counsellor can take to enhance the child's autonomy and responsibility, and avoid a tendency towards becoming confrontational:

1 Encourage the child to talk about his concerns and convey interest and respect. Seek clarification without trying to understand a situation too quickly. Prompts such as: 'Help me to understand …' and 'Can you say more about what happened when …' facilitate this.
2 Adopt a 'one-down' position to avoid becoming confrontational or seeming to be all-knowing. The role of 'consultant' is far preferable to the one of 'expert' or authority figure.

3   Acknowledge indifference or diffidence. There are few things worse in counselling than the counsellor persisting with 'What's the problem?' questions when the client quite obviously is still not convinced that he even wants to be there. A simple statement from the counsellor can help to lighten the atmosphere and remove an impasse to talking about the client's issues. This might be phrased as follows:

> Brandon, I guess it's not easy coming here because your teacher sent you. And you say that you'd rather be in the school gym with your friends. That's OK to feel that way. But since Mr Thompson sent you and expects us to get our heads around some issue or concern, let's use this time as best we can. Even if this turns out to be a one-off meeting. How does that sound to you?

4   Take the child's perspective and work with this. Although someone else might have referred the child or labelled them as having a particular problem, work with the child's ideas and experiences and try to put to the side those communicated by others not present.

5   Be practical and try to solicit simple solutions from the child in the first instance. At some point, the child will expect to see some practical resolution to his problem and a hint of this possibility in the first session is helpful for engaging a reluctant child. For example:

> Tony, we've spent a lot of time focusing on your worries about taking exams. Is there one small thing that you might do – or do differently – to make it easier on yourself?

6   Praise and validate the child when appropriate. For example:

> OK, so your friends called you a 'poof' for going to see the counsellor. But maybe it takes a special strength and an ability to sometimes go against the flow to talk to a stranger about a personal issue.

We do not wish to give the view that engaging a reluctant client is a simple matter of uttering a few of the 'right' sentences. Our own experiences of occasional failures are testimony to this. However, it would be wrong to conclude this section on a note that conveys that all adolescents are problematic and sometimes troublesome. Nothing could be further from the truth and this is not borne out in research. Jeffrey Arnett, a psychologist at the University of Maryland College Park, published an outstanding paper (Arnett, 1999) in which he reviewed the concept of 'adolescent storm and stress'. He stated: 'For the most part, contemporary psychologists reject the view that adolescent storm and stress is universal and inevitable' (p.317). While not discounting that adolescence is a difficult time for both the individual and their family, he asserts that higher rates of conflict in families during adolescence 'does not indicate a serious or enduring breach in parent–adolescent relationships … parents and adolescents tend to report that overall their relationships are good' (p.320). We quote directly from this paper because the points covered are central to our own experiences of working with adolescents, and these underpin some of the ideas described in this book. Conflict in relationships is almost inevitable during adolescence. Managed well, these perturbations may steadily decrease and the passage to adulthood can be smoothed over without lasting damage to significant relationships; if mismanaged, things can go seriously wrong. School counsellors carry significant responsibilities which test all of their clinical skills, as much as their character and ability to remain level headed in unenviable and difficult circumstances.

The objectives of counselling

By engaging in a counselling or psychotherapeutic relationship for self-exploration, many children will be helped to articulate their difficulties and work towards their resolution. Through this process the child is encouraged to move towards openness and self-trust as opposed to feeling either stuck or invalidated. The child or adolescent is helped to gain self-confidence rather than being sub-jected to what others believe he or she ought to be.

In general, counselling and psychotherapy approaches taught in colleges and universities tend to favour individualistic theories, such as humanistic and psychodynamic approaches. This book was first conceived in an effort to provide counsellors, teachers, family therapists and other allied professionals with a theoretical base and a guide for the practice of counselling in school settings. Our experience of working in different school settings brought our attention to some of the limitations of training and the lack of practical guidelines for counsellors. We felt it would be helpful to describe our ideas about counselling after many years of practice, close collaboration and carrying out and publishing research. The contents of this book describe more fully:

- *a systemic perspective* which takes into account not only the individual child, but also his or her family and the context or setting in which counselling takes place. This is usually the school, but necessity may occasionally require sessions to take place in the family home, or a neutral setting such as the counsellor's practice.
- *the skills and practice of school counselling* against a background of indivi-dual, family and school life, and different manifestations of the problem.
- *a framework for school counselling* based on a tried and tested approach that has been used for several years in different school settings.
- *a framework or map* which the counsellor can use with confidence when responding to diverse problems, one which can be applied with a good measure of flexibility.

Beliefs about the psychological care of children within the school setting

This book describes the tasks of counsellors working in school settings and some of the beliefs that inform our practice. These beliefs, which influence our approach to counselling, come from our experience of working with children in schools and with different groups, such as teachers and families. The ideas also come from the authors' training in and experience of using different, although complementary, counselling approaches. The main therapeutic approaches which inform our practice are: family-systems, solution-focused, cognitive-behavioural and attachment theories. Some of these beliefs – also described in the previous chapter – can be summarised as follows:

- It is helpful to recognise that problems can arise for individuals at different points in their school career, or pre-existing psychological problems can be exacerbated by different stressful experiences, e.g. friendship issues, bullying, family breakdown, sickness, death of loved ones, underage sex, gay and lesbian relationships, anorexia, drugs and overload of schoolwork, to name but a few.
- These problems have implications for relationships and attachments between the children, family members and teachers.
- The 'family' is the child's most important social system. Our definition of family incorporates not only blood relatives but also close social relationships.
- It is important to be mindful of both the social context of the child and the context in which counselling is provided. Context gives meaning to the psychological problem and, to a large extent, determines the range of possible solutions to it.
- School settings are different from the traditional counselling setting. There is a different pace to the work and different views about confidentiality, working practices, length of sessions and duration of counselling. It is essential to be adaptable and to respect the demands and constraints of school settings.
- There are many approaches to counselling which can be used to equal effect. Whichever approach is used, a 'map' helps to conceptualise problems and their possible resolution.
- It is useful to have clear goals and objectives for counselling sessions in school settings. These can be linked to the definition of the problem (or changes in the definition of the problem), considering for whom it is a problem and a plan for working towards a resolution. There need be no predetermined or inflexible ideas about what would be the best solution in a particular case. However, an understanding of psychotherapeutic theory guides the counsellor in thinking about the onset of the problem, exploring the definition of the problem and formulating possible solutions.
- Lack of training in psychological theories or vague theoretical ideas can lead to confusion in counselling sessions for both the pupil and counsellor.
- The counsellor's task is to help the pupil identify what meaning the problems have for them and to discuss the consequences of them. The concern must be to avoid situations in which the child may feel pushed to see things in the way the counsellor sees them, or where the counsellor inadvertently disqualifies his ideas or feelings.
- In some circumstances, counsellors may have to explain their actions to others in a court of law and professional supervision, theory and research may be important aspects of this.

• Lastly, the child is encouraged to collaborate in the process of counselling. This is a major departure from the traditional hierarchical configuration in counselling in which the counsellor is seen to have power and control. It is not akin to a relationship with a parent figure. One consequence is that counsellors now have to accept greater challenges and more uncertainty in their practice. Some may also find the practice of this approach less stressful and more rewarding as responsibility is shared with the child.

A definition of counselling

By now, the reader should have some understanding of the objectives of solution-focused systemic counselling in schools. However, we have still to define what we mean by 'counselling'. Counselling is not a process of 'doing something to someone'. It is best described as an interactive process. Although there are many definitions of counselling and psychotherapy, it is necessary to clarify our definition:

> Counselling is an interaction in a therapeutic setting, focusing primarily on a conversation about relationships, beliefs and behaviour (including feelings), through which the child's perceived problem is elucidated and framed or reframed in a fitting or useful way, and in which new solutions are generated and the problem takes on a new meaning.

Our definition is intentionally broad so as to take into account the fact that helping people in a therapeutic context does not necessarily imply finding solutions to their problems, but can provide a relationship where they can be helped to feel understood and better about themselves and their problem. Another important point is that the relationship between the counsellor and the child is a collaborative one. It is not hierarchical, nor is it necessarily didactic. It takes into account the fact that the counsellor is viewed as a specialist in therapeutic skills, but that the child also has some expertise in the issues and problems that concern them. It is through collaboration between counsellor and child (and other professionals) that positive outcomes in counselling are best achieved.

How can counselling help children in a school setting?

Counselling can help children to:

• examine the difficulties or problems they are experiencing and gain insight into what factors maintain these difficulties;
• facilitate decision making;
• discuss difficulties in relationships and how to cope with them;
• identify useful coping strategies that the child already has and enhance these;

- identify existing sources of support that may facilitate coping but are not being used, including peer, family and other professional support;
- gain insight into practical techniques that they can use to deal with their problem;
- explore and challenge perceptions of poor body image and low self-esteem.

What actually happens in counselling?

There are many myths about what actually happens in counselling sessions. Some people may expect to see a leather couch and to be greeted by a bearded Freud-like figure asking them to talk about their mother! This is now rarely the case and modern approaches to counselling are often focused, short term and effective. Most counsellors are concerned with helping children to feel safe and comfortable in the counselling sessions so they can explore their problems with a view towards their resolution. This involves several stages including: introducing the concept of counselling to the child; addressing any concerns that they may have about being in the session; identifying for whom the problem is most a problem, and exploring difficulties; finding out how the child has so far attempted to solve the problem; and monitoring changes in the child, the problem and significant relationships. Figure 2.1 outlines some of the main stages of the counselling process.

In spite of advances in the modern practice of counselling, some people are still often concerned about the stigma attached to seeing a counsellor. It is therefore a good idea first to explore with the child his or her views and expectations about counselling. An over-emphasis on counselling in school settings may inadvertently cause some children, parents, or even teachers to believe there is a psychological problem. Indeed, another distinguishing factor of the school setting is that it is a non-pathologising context unlike, for example, working in a health-care setting. The theoretical aim of the school is to promote the well-being of the child. Counselling can contribute to making this happen. This can often be best achieved in terms of shifting the conversation into the future tense which is a characteristic of working with a solution-focused systemic approach (see Chapter 4). It is the domain of childhood to have ideas, plans and aspirations for the future. To open up a conversation about such plans can contribute not only to shifting the focus so that the conversation is about the problem, but also can powerfully endorse any change and contribute to the construction of future possibilities.

Counsellor:	Now that you've discovered family relationships valuable and supportive for you since the time of the car accident and the injuries you've sustained, how does this influence your plans for the future?
Tom:	Without a doubt, I'm going to a university that is close to home. I shall live in the students' residence, but I'll know that the people who really understand my difficulties will be readily at hand should I need them. My family are very happy with this too.

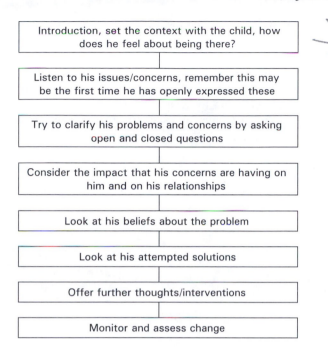

FIGURE 2.1   *Main stages of the counselling process*

The approach described in this book starts out from the premise that problems first need to be identified and defined by the child, family or teachers. An assumption on the part of the counsellor that all children with problems will benefit from counselling is unfounded. This view can be detrimental to the child, the position of the counsellor in the system, and to how others view the practice of counselling. Many potential psychological problems in school settings are noticed and dealt with within the normal day-to-day running of the school.

Conversational and problem-solving skills are highly relevant in school settings. However, there is some difference between being a counsellor on the one hand and having counselling skills on the other. Almost all teachers will counsel at some time during the course of their work. They constantly interact with children, helping them to adjust to new and sometimes unwelcome situations. Psychotherapists, counsellors, and psychologists are expected to have advanced training and qualifications in their field. The problems that arise in school settings may challenge people's existing counselling maps or frameworks. This book attempts to address some of these issues, conveying an approach to counselling children in school settings that has been applied and developed in several school settings through a range of social and personal problems.

Conclusion

No counselling approach described in published literature teaches one 'what to say when'. Instead, counsellors and trainees in counselling can be introduced to new (either more or less expansive) ways of examining psychological problems and can incorporate an ever-widening range of concepts and skills in their practice map. The ideas in this book are not specifically intended to challenge a counsellor's preferred counselling approach – be it Kleinian, Jungian, client-centred, cognitive, behavioural, systemic, or any other. The aim is to extend the repertoire of ideas and skills available to counsellors and to enhance their practice by reflecting on some of the unique and specific challenges of working as a counsellor in a school setting.

3   Theory of Solution-Focused Counselling in the School Setting

Some conceptual ideas about practising as a counsellor in a school setting are described in this chapter. An ability to approach each new case and problem with a receptive openness and to recognise that each child will require different therapeutic approaches and procedures is necessary. This attitude needs to be balanced with a level of competence in tried and tested counselling approaches and interventions.

The approaches favoured in this book are underpinned by systemic and solution-focused theoretical principles. We describe a solution-focused counselling approach which has been found well suited to working in school settings. A solution-focused approach is useful for understanding the context of the evolution, maintenance and resolution of psychological problems. Working with this approach implies working within a set of beliefs which assert that:

- time is limited;
- every session might be the last;
- there should be less preoccupation with problems and more on the construction of possibilities that lead to a resolution of those problems;
- the child's resources, competencies, skills, strengths and coping abilities should be sought throughout the session;
- the objective is not necessarily to fix or cure the problem (though this is always a welcome outcome), but rather to help children out of the position in which they find themselves;
- the relationship between child and counsellor should be co-operative;
- goals arising from the session should be devised jointly.

This approach therefore ensures that attempts to treat psychological problems do not inadvertently lead to their exacerbation or jeopardise the position of the counsellor in the school setting. We use an integrative counselling method, drawing on ideas from complementary frameworks of systemic theory and practice. We endeavour to be flexible and responsive to the ideas and beliefs of the child, his family and his teachers.

Progress in counselling in schools can be jeopardised by: (a) a lack of skills or insufficient understanding of psychotherapeutic theory; (b) persistence with an idea or intervention in spite of feedback from the child (and/or his social or family system) that this is not helpful; (c) inattention to the difficulties of the counsellor's role in relation to the family and teachers.

Counselling and psychotherapy can imply weekly or more frequent sessions with a trained counsellor over many years. Clearly this is inappropriate for a school setting. In addition, while this may be necessary or helpful for some children, there is a requirement for briefer periods of contact with the counsellor. Indeed, effective solution-focused counselling can sometimes be conducted in a single session.

Core theoretical concepts for counsellors working in school settings

We have identified 11 main theoretical concepts for the counsellor which reflect the unique and specific features of therapeutic work in school settings. These are derived from different theories of counselling and psychotherapy (including psychodynamic, systemic, person-centred, cognitive-behavioural and personal construct, among others) and our own personal experience. The considerations listed below also act as a summary of some of the key points already raised and are as follows:

1   Psychosocial approach

The application of a psychosocial approach (integrating psychological and social features) to counselling has been extensively illustrated by McDaniel et al. (1992). There is a need for the counsellor to work collaboratively and without undue emphasis on either psychological or social processes (to the detriment of the other). Social and psychological events and processes are viewed as being interconnected and each requires the ongoing attention of the counsellor. There is sometimes a tendency to overemphasise social processes, whereas psychological events may be equally relevant, and vice versa.

2   Context

It is important to understand the context in which problems are identified or dealt with. The setting or context may be in the classroom, in private with a teacher, with the mother, the father, or a combination. Each will influence or constrain the amount of time available for the child, the degree of privacy in counselling sessions and sometimes also the psychotherapeutic approach used. The context determines how problems are viewed, what can be done about them and who should be involved in dealing with them. Systemic counsellors have been closely associated with the development and application of the contextual therapies and conceptual ideas pertaining to counselling and context advanced by Selvini Palazzoli and her co-workers (1980a).

3   Beliefs

Beliefs about the correct way to behave in certain environments, how to react to situations and how the parents' standards differ from the school's may affect how a child responds to his therapy and how he is likely to cope. The cognitive-behavioural and personal construct approaches emphasise the relevance of cognitions and beliefs in the onset, maintenance and treatment of psychological problems. Wright et al. (1996) distinguish between constraining and facilitative beliefs. Constraining beliefs maintain problems and impede the search for new options or alternatives. Facilitative beliefs expand possibilities for solutions. Beliefs are directly linked to behaviour. If a child does not believe, for example, that it is wrong to retaliate to taunts from other children, then he will be less likely to comply to the suggestion that he should turn the other cheek.

4 Attachment

The connection between attachment anxieties to parents in childhood and psychological problems helps us to understand how people relate to one another. For example, a child may be causing problems in school because he desires the attention that is lacking in his family life; or he may be withdrawn at school because he is scared of initiating interactions which, when he is at home, result in conflict. John Byng-Hall (1995) has provided a solid foundation for understanding attachment in human relationships, especially in the context of changing family relationships.

5 Typology of the problem

An understanding of the main characteristics of a problem is important in order to determine the cause of the problem and how the child may feel about it. It is not necessary to know about everything in the child's past, but it is desirable to appreciate the time phase and scale of the problem and the consequences that it may have to his schooling.

6 Development and life cycle

Developmental and life-cycle issues determine how the child, the family and siblings are affected by the problem. For the child, this will depend on whether he is an infant, child or adolescent. Parents and families also progress through a series of developmental phases and each may imply or lead to changes in relationships between members of the familial unit. A newly wed couple, older parents or reconstituted family may each be affected differently in response to the child's problem.

7 Curiosity and questions

Counselling proceeds in many different ways. Reflection and interpretation are probably most commonly associated with the process of counselling. However, the counselling interview, using carefully thought-out questions, provides an important source of information for the counsellor (Tomm, 1987). Questions are a main catalyst for change and solutions. Different types of questions can be used to link comments on behaviour, beliefs, feelings and ideas about the future. The purpose of such questions is to heighten the counsellor's sense of curiosity (Cecchin, 1987) and to avoid becoming judgemental or having a fixed view of the child and the problem, rather than a desire to uncover a single 'truth'. Adopting a questioning approach, furthermore, ensures that the child's issues are kept at the forefront of the counselling process. Circular, reflexive and hypothetical or future-oriented questions provide the child and his family with the opportunity to view themselves in the context of relationships and to recognise different perspectives of the problem. The use of questions in counselling in schools is described more fully in Chapter 4.

8   Language, narratives and meanings

Narrative therapy, which draws on the language and stories of the child, helps to reveal meanings about problems and how problems come to be viewed as such. It can be used when working with a whole range of problems. The narrative approach avoids stigmatising or blaming the child and also uses language to help resolve or alleviate problems. Different groups of professionals are taught to think about psychological problems in different and seemingly incompatible ways. Problems are often conceptualised differently by counsellors, psycho-therapists and family therapists, as they are by teachers, families, friends and others involved in the social circle of the child.

9   Cognition and behaviour

The direct (and circular) relationship between cognition (thought) and behaviour (action) is central to an understanding of how problems are maintained and can be resolved. Many psychological problems can be effectively treated with cognitive-behavioural therapy (Beck, 1976). Cognitive-behavioural therapy is especially useful when treating patients suffering from anxiety, depression, insomnia and other problems. Identifying experiences such as dysfunctional assumptions, critical incidents, negative automatic thoughts and other factors which may maintain the problem are the first steps towards resolution. Thinking errors or cognitive distor-tions are often implicated in mood-related problems. For children referred to coun-selling because of separation from one of his parents due to divorce, behavioural methods (such as desensitisation) can be used to ameliorate some symptoms.

10   Time and timing

There may be stringent time constraints within the school setting. Long-term coun-selling approaches may be neither desirable nor feasible in this context where the child cannot regularly attend counselling sessions over a prolonged period. Counsellors who work in school settings may be required to be flexible and impro-vise, thereby remaining responsive to the child's needs. Decisions have to be made about which problems can be dealt with and the duration of counselling.

The challenge in the school setting is for the counsellor either to work quickly and intensively, or more slowly and cautiously. It is important to keep in mind how the child, family and school view progress and outcome in counselling, as this will influence whether the child continues with the sessions and whether the counsellor continues to receive referrals from the school. Some constraints may also relate to the physical setting, such as a lack of privacy or nowhere to sit comfortably with the child, and these may affect when sessions can be arranged and how long they last. We work with a positive attitude of making the most out of every moment and this is characteristic of the approach described in the book. It also specifically suits the school context as it can intensify the counselling process, leading to more rapid results.

11   *Eliciting competence, strength and personal resources*

A characteristic of this approach is working hard with the child to uncover and bring to the surface his resources, strengths, skills, capabilities and coping abilities. These may have temporarily slipped from view as the child struggles to cope with a problem that may either seem overwhelming or even defeating. The fact is that no matter how complex and difficult a situation may be, everyone has a track record of successful problem solving and competence in several, if not many, areas. The task of the counsellor is to restore and highlight this from the outset so as to change the emotional climate of the setting to one of hope and possibility rather than pathology, without denying the pain that the child may be experiencing.

The titles of 'counsellor' or 'psychotherapist' are largely interchangeable. Professional training, the preferences of other colleagues and the tasks under-taken may influence which professional title or 'hat' is chosen. It is reasonable to argue that in school settings all counselling work involves psychotherapy, or vice versa. However, those trained to only undertake information-giving and implications counselling should not treat children using psychotherapeutic approaches and techniques without further training and supervision. Untrained and unsupervised counsellors may be ineffective or even damaging to the child.

Application of a systemic approach to counselling

Traditional models of counselling have an individual orientation. Indications of problems are looked for *inside* the person and counselling is directed exclusively at the person as the intervention target. A solution-focused systemic approach encourages the counsellor to look beyond the apparent problem and consider the wider social context of the child when assessing or treating them. A basic tenet of the solution-focused systemic approach is that all behaviour is part of an inter-active process, whether at home, at school, or in a counselling session. This is in accordance with the general systems theory, which emphasises the constant con-tact of people with their external environment; that no one is isolated or protected from outside influences. It is important to note that this interaction is especially

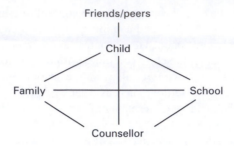

FIGURE 3.1   *Constellation of relationships*

salient with children as it occurs at a time of developmental changes. Key areas in which change will manifest include relationships with friends, peers, family members, teachers and oneself. The counsellor should always keep in mind the following minimum constellation of relationships when working in a school setting (Figure 3.1).

Taking the idea of a constellation further, we are led to the notion of causal links between the child, the family and the school. Not only do the behaviours and actions of the family and school affect the child, but the subsequent behaviours and actions of the child in turn affect the family and the school (Dowling and Osborne, 1994). Linear causality is replaced by the concept of circular causality. For example, if a child breaks a school rule, the school may react by punishing him according to their regulations. There is then the possibility that certain teachers in the school will remember the child for having broken that rule. This may change the teachers' perceptions of the child and therefore cause them to treat him differently from the other children, leading him to 'get a name for himself'. This new, less tolerant behaviour from the teachers may lead to the child purposely rebelling against them. The family may also be brought into the equation, either by the child complaining about the situation at home or by the school feeling it necessary to bring it to the parents' attention. Depending on their opinions of the rule and the school, the family may choose to take a side in the matter. Which side they take will influence the view of the school and child towards them.

If we take the above example a stage further, we can envisage a situation where the child has taken on the mantle of being 'difficult' or 'bad'. This role is then reinforced by the changed perceptions and assumptions of the school and maybe the family. This is explained through general systems theory by the concept of homeostasis. In labelling one child as 'bad', the school is able to hold that child up as an example to the rest of 'how not to behave', thus enabling them to maintain the status quo.

It is clear from this that there may be cases where a problem is exacerbated by a lack of communication between the family and the school. The reasons for this may be obvious (that the family has little faith in the school and chooses not to accept their opinions of the child), or hidden from view (that teachers' morale is low and this is having an effect on their work and relationship with pupils).

Whatever the reasons and opinions of each system, it is necessary to emphasise the fact that families and schools are part of a dynamic two-way relationship. Their attitudes towards each other will affect the attitudes of the child. This should be taken into consideration by any counsellor entering the situation. Indeed, the counsellor may be the only one in the school system who is the recipient of all viewpoints. Hence the possibility exists that she may be able to facilitate the exchange of information between the school and the parents and contribute to challenging entrenched attitudes. Behaviour cannot be studied in isolation, without taking into account the situation in which it occurs. The counsellor may influence the child whose reactions, in turn, have an effect on the counsellor.

An important distinction needs to be made between professional work with the child (counselling) and others involved in the everyday life of the child (family and school). Counselling in school settings should always involve both. This is a basic tenet of a systems perspective. A minimum of three systems is involved in dealing with a school problem at any one time: child, family and school. The participation of a counsellor and the inclusion of the problem as a part of the interactional system results in a more comprehensive depiction of transactions between the child, the family, the school, the problem and the counsellor.

Using this framework helps to avoid the notion that a human problem is discrete, either physical or psychosocial. Instead, all problems are viewed as having biopsychosocial consequences. Psychosocial problems have physical components or features and physical problems have psychosocial ramifications. For example, if a child is unwell, this may affect his general conduct and behaviour at school. Similarly, if the child feels depressed, he may be more likely to complain of physical symptoms such as headaches or feeling unwell. Liaison with both the family and school is needed to ensure that problems (and solutions) are managed collaboratively. Providers of care, including counsellors, are viewed as part of, rather than apart from, the treatment system. This directly challenges the view that counsellors can remain neutral observers, detached from the psychological process. In these settings, counsellors may be confronted with complex interactions between different members of the system which develop into an intense emotional climate.

Similarities between the family and school systems

Both the family and the school are viewed by the child as figures of authority. If there are differences in the way they display and preserve this authority then there is a danger that the child will become confused as to who is 'right' and who is 'wrong'. The family and school are both organised hierarchically. There is a distinct generational gap between those in charge and those who have to adhere to boundaries set by the systems. This may cause the child to question who makes the decisions – the family or the school. The answer to this question is obviously 'both', but inherent in this is the problem that, if the decisions are contradictory, which one should the child question.

When the child starts to think about which rules should be obeyed, there is again the possibility of potential pitfalls. By the time they go to school, children should already know and understand the family rules. Once they start going to school, there is a new set of rules which they can compare and contrast with the original. The family may therefore start to see an integrated version of their rules and the new extra-familial rules that the child has found it necessary to learn and observe.

Families each have their own individual belief system and culture consisting of the language they use, their routines, rituals and shared attitudes towards certain situations or happenings. The belief system will partly determine the culture of the system. Schools, as institutions, also show these cultural differences; for example, Christianity being the usual religion of morning assembly, the mode of address pupils are expected to use when interacting with teachers, and the form that punishments will take.

When problems arise

The counsellor should bear in mind the fact that disagreements or anomalies between the family and school, school and child, and child and family could be a source of potential problems for the child. These problems may take a number of forms. If, for example, the school has difficulty running as a cohesive unit, there may be rivalries between individual teachers or departments, feelings of despair and confusion among the staff and a lack of communication between staff and parents. This may cause the counsellor to ask herself a number of questions:

- Is the adult–child relationship based on negative feelings between both parties?
- Is the relationship 'stuck' because of inflexible attitudes?
- Have I taken all viewpoints into consideration?
- Do I have an equal relationship with all parties?
- Are these factors preserving the child's behaviour?

Thus it is seen that the interactions of groups can have a profound effect on the behaviour of an individual. Psychological problems must always be considered in the light of the child's social context. Behaviour should not be interpreted in isolation of the child's relationships as it is within his ecology of relationships that the counsellor will come to understand the relevance or meaning of his actions, however abnormal they may appear. People do not simply react to situations; they evaluate and interpret what is going on and how this affects them and this helps us to broaden our view of a child's behaviour and problem. A child's behaviour, although seemingly abnormal, may be a perfectly normal reaction to a stressful situation. For example:

- The parents are having difficulty with another sibling.
- The family and school are sending out conflicting signals.
- The school has a preconceived notion of the child's behaviour that the child does not understand.
- The child's parents are separating.

In situations such as these, the child will naturally feel anxious, rejected or confused. It is necessary to concentrate on the needs of the child as well as focusing on the evident problems of the family and school systems. The counsellor should therefore ask himself the following questions:

- Who referred the child to the counsellor?
- How does the school/family/child perceive the problem?
- How willing is the school/family/child to be involved in counselling?
- What are the attitudes of the school/family/child towards the other parties?
- What resources are available to help the school/family/child?
- What are the strengths and weaknesses of the school/family/child?
- How well does the school/family run as a system?
- Have there been any changes in the school/family systems in the last few months that could have caused the problem?

Asking these questions and others like them will allow the counsellor constantly to hone her understanding of the situation and enable her to continue to make original suggestions where others have a set view of the problem. Working with such a questioning approach also contributes to creating an atmosphere where responsibility for problem resolution is shared between child, parents, school and counsellor. This, in turn, will facilitate development of possible solutions to the problem.

Interventions for change

As has already been shown, it is always necessary to consider all the systems involved in the development and maintenance of a problem. As Anderson et al. (1986: 8) note: 'The definition of a problem marks the context and therefore the boundaries of the system to be treated ... the problem to be diagnosed and treated and the membership of the problem system is determined by those in active communication regarding the problem.'

The emphasis of the solution-focused systemic approach is communication. If the family, child and school all talk to each other, it will be easier to ascertain where differences of approach and perception lie. A lack of communication can not only maintain a problem, but also exacerbate it if responsibility is not taken. The emphasis should be on the negotiation of common ground and discussion of possible resolutions, as opposed to overconcentration on the problem itself. Realisation of these resolutions will enable the family, school, child and counsellor to define specific plans that will lead towards change. There are a number of different ways of intervening:

- individual sessions with the child;
- joint meetings with the family and teacher in order to work towards solving difficulties in the school;
- helping school staff develop communication skills to aid the sharing of knowledge with children and their families;

- bringing the parents into the school for joint meetings with the child;
- if appropriate, visiting parents in the family home, emphasising treatment and change within the family;
- a collaborative approach with the child, family and school.

The counsellor should always ask herself the following questions:

- Who do I want to attend the session?
- Who would be willing to attend the session?
- Where shall we meet?

Approaching each problem from a unique perspective will allow the counsellor to develop an individual solution for dealing with that specific problem. The counsellor should ensure that no assumptions are made about each case before the facts are presented by each individual and system involved. This will allow for a fresh solution to be sought every time a problem is encountered.

Objectivity

It is important to be sensitive to each member of each system, be they a child, a parent or a teacher. During the discussion of problems, it is likely that an appeal will be made to the counsellor's 'sensibility'. There is no harm in acknowledging when an appropriate observation has been made, but the counsellor must ensure not to create an inadvertent alliance with one system in favour of another. If the counsellor is seen as siding with, for example, the family, this may cause difficulties as the school may feel that they are unable to trust the counsellor. The counsellor should facilitate and, if necessary, steer discussion, but should never try to influence or turn people against each other. Everybody should be made to feel that the counsellor has sympathy with his or her point of view.

Information sharing is also a necessary part of the therapeutic process. Counselling sessions provide an ideal opportunity for non-communicative groups to understand each other's intentions and perspectives. However, it is essential that anything shared in confidence with the counsellor is respected as personal and not for discussion with others.

A distinct benefit of the solution-focused systemic approach is the opportunity that the counsellor has to interact with all those involved in the problem. The counsellor is able to forge positive relationships with the family and school and offer understanding and support to them. It is absolutely imperative that nothing is done which could potentially jeopardise these relationships.

Conclusion

Different theoretical approaches contribute complementary ideas to the practice of counselling in school settings. The emphasis in counselling should be on developing an integrative approach which brings together different ideas and skills in a unifying conceptual framework, rather than an eclecticism which may seem confusing or muddled in practice. The approach described in this book emphasises brief counselling. Experience has taught us to be receptive to ideas developed outside our main theoretical framework and to integrate these into our practice.

4 Aims and Structure of the Counselling Session

This chapter focuses on translating some theoretical ideas into counselling practice. Effective counselling about problems in school settings needs clarity of purpose. To help achieve clarity, a framework is described which includes the principles and aims of counselling. In addition, having a 'map' or structure for the session can make it easier to achieve the tasks. This map can lead to:

- better use of counselling sessions;
- fewer misunderstandings about how counselling can help;
- increased satisfaction with counselling;
- a clearer set of criteria against which the efficacy of counselling can be evaluated.

Theoretical concepts

The approach to counselling described here has been adapted from the techniques of the Milan Associates (Palazzoli et al., 1980a, 1980b) which enables the counsellor to develop a map of therapeutic practice. A salient feature of this approach is the *structure* to the counselling session, which helps to ensure that important issues are addressed in the context of school settings.

Use of questions

As the session develops, the exact order of the steps depends on the flow of conversation, which is guided by questions. Questions facilitate the process between the child and counsellor and help to achieve a structure to the session. These questions:

- help to keep a focus;
- explore ideas or hypotheses about the problem;
- avoid making assumptions about people and their relationships;
- identify knowledge, concerns and wishes;
- rank concerns and wishes;
- help people to be specific by clarifying the meaning of what is said; for example: 'You say you are depressed. Can you say more about that? How does it show?'

- link people with ideas and other people they had not previously considered;
- address and inform about unfamiliar and sensitive issues.

A range of questions may be relevant to the counselling situation:

1 *Linear questions* usually lead to 'yes' or 'no' answers. Under some circum-stances their use is appropriate, but they do not readily open up ideas for discussion. For example: 'Do you think that you have a problem with your class teacher?'

2 *Questions that show a difference* between the present, past and future help people to make connections over time. For example: 'How have you coped with these problems in the past? How do you think you might manage in the future, and how might you cope right now?'

3 *Hypothetical, future-oriented questions* address future concerns and help to explore perceptions of others by linking ideas that might not otherwise have been considered. They are useful in helping people to address difficulties and prepare for the future, while the reality of these situations is some distance away. For example: 'If you still had these problems in two months' time, what would be your main concern? Who would help most, or who or what might make it more difficult?'

4 *Circular questions* link ideas, beliefs and relationships in a way that helps people to view problems from different perspectives or reference points. For example: 'What do you think your mother might most want to discuss today? Would it be the same or different to what you would choose?' Or perhaps 'Where did you get the idea that you always have to take the opposite stance to your teacher?'

5 *Reflective questions* help to reframe problems, allow the counsellor to gain time and the child to glimpse another perspective. For example: 'So you and your mother might see yourself as protecting your father by not telling him that you are here today. Can you say more about that?'

Guiding principles for focused counselling

Guiding principles form a theoretical background to practice and help to focus on the tasks. They include:

- recognising that there are different theoretical approaches. None are neces-sarily right or wrong, but some will be more relevant and applicable in school settings and to certain problems than others;
- avoiding making assumptions about the child's knowledge, concerns, possi-ble reactions or views about the situation;
- having small, achievable goals, overall and for each session – this increases the likelihood of the counsellor and child agreeing about which issues are being dealt with and whether progress is being made;

- using language carefully, as everything said during a session and in interactions with children has an impact and may alter perceptions and responses;
- accepting that the child cannot be completely reassured about a large number of issues, even though certainty and reassurance may be sought from the counsellor;
- being realistic about the child's problem, what can be achieved from a counselling point of view and the counsellor's availability;
- seeking regular consultation and supervision to enhance skills, avoid burnout, audit practice and determine effectiveness.

Aims of counselling

The *aims* of counselling are sometimes confused with its *tasks*. The aims give a broad, as well as defined, purpose to the counselling tasks. The tasks are the steps taken to achieve the aims and may involve the use of various techniques (reframing, creating balance, reducing anxiety to manageable proportions). The aims of counselling can be specific to a particular setting or tasks, but also encompass the more general aims of counselling in school settings. Clarity about the aims of counselling helps to:

- develop a relationship with the child by not raising false expectations about what counselling can achieve;
- dispel misunderstandings (such as that counselling is a friendship relationship);
- reduce myths about what may happen in the sessions.

The aims must always be appropriate for the particular context. Inappropriate, vague, all-encompassing or diffuse aims are less likely to lead to a satisfactory outcome for the child, and the counsellor is more likely to feel that the goals for the session have not been achieved. The main aims for the counsellor include the following:

1 Establish rapport with the child through a dialogue (talk, listen and note what is *not* said).
2 Lead the session by:

- starting the conversation
- keeping a focus when confronted by difficult or challenging situations
- closing the session when it seems appropriate.

3 Elicit and give information by establishing:

- what the child *wants* to know
- their views and wishes in relation to the school and family.

4 Define the problem, explore its implications and consider how counselling can help address the issues that emerge.

5   Identify concerns and issues of importance to the child by helping them to talk about their concerns.

6   Consider relationships with family, friends and the school:

- Who else knows about the problem?
- Who might be most affected, and in what way?

7   Assess the severity of the child's concerns and his social and psychological state by reviewing:

- what the child has said, how he has reacted
- to what extent the problem impacts on the daily life of the child.

8   Help to manage the concerns by helping the child to view his situation from different perspectives, thereby increasing his perceived opinions.

Structuring the counselling session

The following steps construct the 'map' that guides the interview. Although the illustration below is an example of a first session with the child, many of the steps are equally applicable to follow-up contacts. They can also be adapted in style when sessions are held with more than just the child (i.e. the family or the school). The 'map' includes the principles, aims, skills and techniques which are woven into the steps.

1   Think first before the start of each session, in order to anticipate issues and problems for each child. Traditional approaches to counselling define the start of the counselling process as the first meeting between the counsellor and the child. The systemic approach recognises that this process begins when a referral is being considered or discussed. An *hypothesis* is made about the impact of the problems on the child and his relationships, taking into account the stage of life of the child, the child's social and cultural context and the referral.

2   Introduce the session by clarifying:

- who you are
- your task in relation to the child
- the purpose of the meeting
- the time available.

The same procedure should be followed, apart from introductions, in subsequent sessions.

3   Engage the child (build rapport) by asking questions to gain information rapidly about expectations. This helps to focus the discussion on:

- what the child understands about the meeting;
- what he wants to achieve and his expectations for the session;
- who else knows about the problem or that the child is having counselling;
- whether there is anyone he might want to be made aware of his problems.

4   *Give a focus* to the session by setting *small, achievable goals*, for example: 'If there was one thing you wanted to achieve from our meeting today, what might it be?'

5   *Elicit and give information* throughout the session, in different ways, by exploring the extent of the child's knowledge about his problem. Sometimes it is the child who wants information. At other times it is the family, the school or the counsellor who considers that there is information to impart. If the child's knowledge is first explored through questioning, misinformation can be corrected and the gaps in knowledge can be filled at the child's pace. It is useful to check what the child has understood at the end of a period of information giving:

Counsellor: What do you know about dyslexia?
Child: Only a little.
Counsellor: What is the little that you do know?

6   *Identify beliefs* about the problem through questions, for example: 'What is your view about how dyslexia will affect your work?' This question can reveal the child's beliefs and rapidly gives information about the likelihood of compliance with specific guidance.

7   *Identify the child's main concerns early* in sessions to enable the most pressing issues to be addressed in the time available: 'What thoughts do you have about what might happen if your exam nerves prevented you from staying in the examination hall?'

8   *Rank concerns* in order of importance or severity; this

- reduces anxiety to manageable proportions;
- helps the child to be specific;
- helps to set small achievable goals, giving individuals a sense of control.

It is recognised that if problem solving is successfully applied to one issue, it often highlights and gives experiences about how to tackle other difficulties. For example: 'Of all the worries about your problem, who to tell, whether it will annoy your parents and the impact on your schoolwork – which worries you the most?'

9   *Use language carefully* to avoid or reduce misunderstandings. Using the child's own words is a technique which:

- helps the counsellor, when he feels stuck, to gain time and to enter the child's world view: 'You say you are depressed all the time. How much of the time is all the time? Is there ever a time when you are not depressed?'

- builds rapport with the child, because it confirms that he has been heard and helps the counsellor to move at the child's pace: 'You say that you feel depressed. How does that affect you?'
- facilitates the discussion of sensitive or unfamiliar issues, for example: 'You say you are scared of the other children in your class. What scares you most about them?'

10 *Help the child to manage concerns* by:

- reframing problems, enabling them to consider their predicament differently. This may ultimately help them to cope better on a day-to-day basis, while at the same time being realistic about the problem (Box 4.1).

Box 4.1

Case example: taking small steps to make the future more manageable

When faced with an overwhelming sense of loss of future, identifying small, attainable goals can restore to the adolescent some feeling of control over his life. The following case example illustrates how some of these ideas were discussed with Michael, recently diagnosed with HIV, and soon to turn 16 years of age.

Michael: What is the point of staying on at school if I'm going to die?
Counsellor: We don't know when anyone is going to die even if they have AIDS. Supposing you were to live for at least another ten or twenty years, what would you want to do with the time?
Michael: Photography and travel.
Counsellor: Have you thought about how you might achieve this if you decided to leave school now?
Michael: Get a part-time job. I've looked for a job, but there aren't any around.
Counsellor: Would it make it easier to get a job if you stayed longer at school and sat for A levels?
Michael: Probably, but it takes so long.
Counsellor: Have you thought about joining the photography society at school so that you don't need to wait so long before starting to do what you want to do?

- exploring resources available to the child (how he has coped in the past, how he might cope in the future, the possibility of extra tuition);
- engaging the family and school whenever possible (discussions including members of each group in interviews with the child). This also helps to relieve stress on staff and increase the range of useful interventions.

11 Maintain clear boundaries between a professional and a friendship relationship. Enable the session to be therapeutic (the essence of the counselling relationship) by:

- always being thoughtful about the impact of what is said and what happens during the session;
- maintaining a neutral stance (showing no surprise, asking questions). For example: 'You say that you want to leave school altogether? How do you think that might affect your future?' [*in a neutral, matter-of-fact tone*].
- sharing responsibilities with the child (concerns about them) and with the family and school (case discussions and meetings). For example: 'If you do decided to stop going to school, how do you think it might affect you? Who else do you think knows about your feelings? Is there anyone you think should know?'

12 Make an assessment towards the end of the session, based on what has been seen and heard, from emotional, social and behavioural points of view. Hypothetical and future-orientated questions which explore how the child might cope, and who else is around, are especially useful.

13 End the session by summarising the issues discussed. Ending the session well is as important as making a good start at the beginning and includes the following:

- *Decision-making* for the child and the counsellor. The child may have to decide whether or not to come back for more counselling; whether to talk to his family or the school and he may have issues to share with them. The counsellor has to decide whether she is the right person to offer psychological support; who to discuss the problem with in the future; and the intervals between sessions with the child.
- *Summarising* what has been seen and heard, focusing both on identified strengths and weaknesses. If emphasis is only placed on the positive aspects of the situation, it will not be realistic and the child will not be effectively supported. For example: 'From what I've heard and seen today you have several worries, but seem to have people who you could turn to for help. However, there is something stopping you. Maybe you are protecting them. Maybe you are also protecting yourself from feeling dependent or facing up to your problems. It seems that you will know when the time is right to take a move towards getting the support you want.'
- *Indicate what follow-up* there will be, as this reduces the likelihood of unexpected phone calls or visits. If there is to be an ending and no follow-up, this should also be clarified. Details include:
  - who can be contacted between sessions and how this can be done.
  - careful consideration of the time between sessions. For example, if the child is seen too frequently, he could be given the message that he cannot manage alone. If the time between sessions is too long, the threads of help may be weakened.

Working with the family

Thus far in this chapter, the focus has been on working with the individual child and exploring his problem. We now turn our attention to family and relationship dynamics and the unique skills required to work with these. Counsellors have differing views about whether they work with parents as well as children. This is more likely to reflect their skills and confidence in working with couples and families and therefore their theoretical framework. Some counsellors prefer not to work with parents, arguing that this may affect their relationship with the child. However, the solution-focused systemic school counsellor may view working with parents differently. First, no child has a problem in isolation and their family is inevitably affected by it, if not directly implicated in its onset and maintenance. Second, problems can sometimes be more easily and efficiently solved in the context of family meetings. To this end, an engaged family can help to resolve the child's problems. Third, as already discussed, a collaborative approach to counselling enhances the effectiveness of the counsellor by drawing on the influence and resources of others in helping to solve problems. Fourth, consultations with parents may help to prevent problems with the child. For example they may request a meeting with the counsellor in order to discuss how they might respond to a dilemma they have with the child. This may not necessitate ever seeing the child, and a difficulty might be arrested before it turns into an entrenched problem. Fifth, where family dynamics are at the source of the problem, the counsellor will gain a lot in her assessment if she is able to observe and experience the patterns of relationships in the family, and how the child copes in the family context. The counsellor may work with the parents, parents and child, the whole family, or even include a teacher or another colleague at school, where appropriate. Skills for working with couples and families are best acquired through formal training in family therapy.

Family dynamics in the counselling context

Throughout our lives we encounter change. Personal development is punctuated by a series of life stages – birth, infancy, childhood, adolescence and so on – and our ability to communicate progress with each stage. We learn to communicate through social interaction and, primarily, through family life. Social development, including the acquisition and development of language, is intricately related to family development, roles, relationships and transgenerational patterns. How we relate to people and communicate is influenced to a large extent by interaction patterns in our own family. Many factors are relevant in this regard:

- Your position in the family (an only child, the eldest sibling, the youngest, etc.).
- Family rules or beliefs about communication (e.g. 'One has to be an adult to be taken seriously.' 'Children should be seen and not heard.').
- Transgenerational patterns (e.g. only the views of male members are regarded; opinions count only when you have left home; no one speaks about feelings because it is viewed as a sign of weakness).

- The structure of the family (e.g. 'There were so many of us at home that it was difficult to be heard.').
- Legacies from past family events ('Nobody dared question my father ever again after I had a terrible row with him.' 'Only my mother spoke openly about feelings after my brother died in an accident, and a few years ago she became clinically depressed. Now there's an idea in the family that a stiff upper lip in the face of adversity can prevent one from going mad.').

Context is crucial in understanding communication: people's expectations are defined by the context in which they communicate. Behaviour and language are likely to differ depending on the situation. A conversation with friends in the playground will be more relaxed and friendly than a conversation during an interview for a place at school. But context is only one marker of communication. Others include personal and social development which implies change in how we communicate and what is implied by our communications as we move through different stages of life. The transitions to starting school, and from school to university, are for many young people the most significant stages in the process of leaving home. They mark two major changes. The first is in oneself: one becomes more separate and autonomous. The second is in relation to one's family: the family structure may not change, but new patterns in relationships are established. But these changes need not signal the end of relationships or changes in relationships. We may, however, relate differently.

At times of emotional distress, we often look to others for support and may depend more on our close family and friends. But social support is not only concerned with practical problems, such as getting to and from school or making sure that homework is done. It also entails emotional support and comfort at a time when hope and self-confidence may wane. Studies have shown that social support can act as a buffer to psychological distress. There is also evidence that our bodies undergo physiological changes at stressful times such as the loss of a partner, close friend or relative. Social support therefore can have an impact on both psychological and physical health. For this reason we must take care to help children sustain important relationships at times of distress and encourage them to draw support from others.

Most school counsellors are trained to work with individuals and consequently focus in counselling sessions on intrapsychic processes, self-beliefs and the child's feelings. When working in school settings, issues pertaining to emotional, social and practical support, and the impact of problems on the family and the school, are also highly relevant. A genogram, also known as a family tree, pedigree or genealogical chart, is a clinical tool used for acquiring, storing and processing information about family history, composition and relationships in counselling sessions. A genogram can be used to develop a map of family relationships with the child and identify sources of support within the family. Genograms have been used in psychotherapy for years and are a natural fit for counselling in school settings (see Appendix E).

The information contained in a genogram may include medical, behavioural, genetic, cultural and social aspects of the family system. This information can provide a rich source of hypotheses with regard to how a problem may be linked to family history and relationships and how it may evolve through time. Genograms help to reveal patterns and events which may have recurring significance within a family system. McGoldrick and Gerson (1985) explain that the act of constructing a family diagram or genogram with a child or family, to map relationships and functioning patterns, acts in a way similar to language – to potentiate and organise thought processes. To this end, genograms can be conceptualised as both a therapeutic intervention and a part of the process of counselling.

Knowledge of a child's family history and relationships is important in a school setting for several reasons. Information about a child's family background helps in:

- understanding the family's role in the aetiology of the problem;
- identifying psychological problems in different family constellations such as stepfamilies;
- making an assessment of familial, biological and psychiatric disorders (e.g. asthma, schizophrenia);
- understanding the impact of illness in the family;
- helping the child to make informed choices.

A genogram provides an immediate picture of the family and its history. It is a useful alternative to having to search through thick files of notes for biographical and background information. Critical information can be highlighted and current problems considered.

From a systemic persepective, the family life cycle is a crucial variable to consider when counselling, since it will have implications not only for the child, but the family as a whole. In order for an individual to move on to the next stage in the family life cycle (e.g. a parent facing the empty nest after children have left home to go to university), the family must reorganise itself at each pivotal point that it enters in the life cycle. These transitions can be difficult for some families, especially where there is a problem. Indeed, it may be the fear or anxiety surrounding a pending or recent transition that is at the core of the presenting problem. Failure to consider this possibility may result in the child being overly pathologised in counselling, whereas the family or school may need to be more directly considered. The listing of ages, dates and significant family events (i.e. births, deaths, divorces) on a genogram enables the counsellor to examine whether or not life-cycle events occurred within expected parameters (McDaniel et al., 1992). The genogram also allows for important anniversaries to be considered, especially those relating to change and loss within the family. This may be particularly relevant in the case of a death or a suicide within a family or illness relating to distress, even though no conscious connection is made between these events and illness.

Genograms provide more than a quantitative measure through which clinical predictions can be made. They can be employed as a means of subjectively interpreting information about relationships and forming tentative hypotheses about the family situation. By obtaining an 'image' of the current family context, the counsellor can assess the family's strengths, as well as the possible links between the presenting problem and family relationships. Individual symptoms can therefore be recast in interpersonal terms. For example, a genogram might help to reveal that the onset of a child's problem coincided with his mother starting an extra-marital relationship. This could lead to bringing the couple together to work with a counsellor to help their son to overcome his problem.

Although the origins of the genogram lie in family therapy, this tool can also be used effectively in counselling, with an individual child, the child with parents and the parents alone. Indeed, it is especially useful in cases where:

- a psychological problem has implications for other family members, but they are not present in counselling;
- the presenting problem appears to stem from family relationships;
- illness and issues of loss need to be addressed in counselling;
- other care-givers seem to have inadvertently maintained or exacerbated the problem;
- the counsellor especially needs to focus on transgenerational patterns and examine (and encourage) coping resources.

Viewing the presenting problem within the context of family relationships and within a multigenerational framework is a powerful way of reframing the problem and removing blame from any one individual. The effect is to normalise the family's understanding of the problem, and perhaps also the reactions of different family members to it. Indeed, once the family patterns which underlie problematic behaviour are identified, it is possible that the behaviour will change without the need for further psychotherapeutic intervention. It is important to note that the whole family does not need to be present to do family work in counselling. Family work can be done with the individual child. It is a matter of focusing on family dynamics and beliefs with the child. This in turn can challenge or alter his own beliefs about family, which in turn may affect how he relates, and hence his own behaviour. Patterns in family relationships are similarly affected. Change in one family member can lead to change in others.

Conclusion

Clarity about the principles and aims of counselling can give counsellors the confidence to focus on the tasks when dealing with the child's problems and their complex effect on the family and the school. Having a structure for the session enables the maximum to be achieved in a relatively short period of time. This can help both those who are trained counsellors and those who use counselling skills as part of their role. When working with children, it is essential to develop skills in exploring the impact of problems in the context of family relationships. This chapter has introduced to the reader the relevance of this to school counselling and highlighted an approach to initiating discussion about the problem and associated impact on relationships.

5 Overview of Essential Counselling Skills

Before we can begin to help children through the use of counselling skills and interventions, we first need to identify and explore their problems. This is an important initial task and we introduce the key concepts in this chapter. A central issue that underscores many of the difficulties which children experience is that there may be some discrepancy between who they perceive themselves to be and who they would like to be. This concept of the 'real' and 'perceived' self and its relationship to the 'ideal' self is an important theme in humanistic counselling (Rogers, 1961). The idea behind this is that the perception that we hold of ourselves is a combination of all the 'I' and 'we' statements that we have heard throughout our lives. By way of contrast, our 'ideal self' is the person that we strive to be. In cases where these two self-perceptions differ, emotional problems may arise. The main task of the counsellor is to empower children to move closer to their ideal self or help them to change their image of their ideal self.

The emphasis in this chapter is on examining the core therapeutic conditions that empower children to address and cope with difficult feelings and problems that they experience. It also includes practical ideas about intervening with problems based on cognitive-behavioural therapy. The core conditions include congruence, unconditional positive regard and empathic understanding (Rogers, 1951).

Box 5.1

Congruence or genuineness

- Implies that the counsellor is 'real' and authentic during the counselling session and conveys interest.
- Suggests that the counsellor's inner experience and non-verbal behaviour are congruent.
- Allows the counsellor openly to express her own feelings.
- Leads to acceptance and the expression of feelings in the session which facilitates honest communication with the child.

Genuineness or congruence should not be misinterpreted as self-disclosure (Box 5.1). A common misconception about genuineness is that the counsellor says exactly what she feels. This may not be helpful as the child may feel invalidated or upstaged. However, it implies that she is aware of what they are feeling and acts consistently with those feelings. Although it is important to be honest with the child, it is also important to keep in mind that expressing your feelings is appropriate only when it facilitates helping the child (Martin, 1989).

Box 5.2

Unconditional positive regard

- Involves expressing a genuine caring for the child.
- Conveys unconditional caring: it is not contaminated by evaluation or judgement of the child's thoughts or feelings.
- The attitude towards the child is not, 'I will accept you when' but rather 'I will accept you as you are'.
- Is the recognition of a child's right to have feelings, though not necessarily the approval of all behaviour.

As in the case of genuineness, the concept of unconditional positive regard is often misconstrued as meaning an overly tolerant permissiveness where no boundaries are set (Box 5.2). This is not the case. Rather, it refers to the fact that the acceptance and positive feelings that the counsellor has for the child are not conditional upon the child's actions or behaviours. Talking to a counsellor who is able to value the child for who he is as a person may be sufficient to help empower him to see himself differently and to make positive changes in his life.

It is important that counsellors do not display shock or embarrassment when they first hear about a child's problems, no matter how distressing and complicated they may seem. Having to summon the courage to attend a counselling session may be difficult enough for a child, without feeling responsible for upsetting the counsellor. This may make it difficult for children to disclose the extent of their despair, or feelings of shame or distress. If the counsellor can convey unconditional positive regard for the child, they will be able to talk about their problem more openly, and not worry about whether or not their feelings are appropriate. The child will then be able to face and examine difficult feelings and issues while still feeling valued as a person, thus validating their experience and feelings.

Box 5.3

Empathic understanding

- Implies that the counsellor will sense the child's feelings as if they were his/her own.
- Goes beyond the recognition of obvious feelings to the level of the less clearly expressed feelings of the child.
- Can help children discuss meanings and experiences about which they may be unaware.

It is important to note that empathy is not sympathy, nor is it about acceptance, liking another person or agreeing with what they have said (Box 5.3). Rather, it is the ability to understand what it is like to be where a person is, to understand what they are saying and to be able to reflect this. An accurate empathic response can help a person to understand and clarify what he or she is feeling and thinking about. A mere reflection or parroting what the child has said may do little to alleviate the child's distress and may come across as condescending or repetitive. Psychologists have devised various methods of assessing the level of empathy in therapeutic reflections. Five levels of empathy described below illustrate how to reflect the child's statements and feelings:

> Client: Since the acne has gotten much worse. I've felt that nothing has gone right. People don't like me. I don't like my work. My relationship with my boyfriend has gone downhill. I don't like who I've become.

A low-level of empathic response could be:

> Counsellor: It sounds like since your acne has gotten worse that things haven't been going well for you.

This response is valid though it does not really attend to what the child has said. It communicates less feeling than the child has expressed. It has not helped the child to gain insight into her experience of having acne. A slightly more empathic response would be:

> Counsellor: So it seems that since it's got worse, the acne has made you feel quite negative about things.

Although this statement conveys an awareness of the surface feelings of the child, it dampens the meaning of what the child has really said. The child here is talking about the way her acne makes her feel and the counsellor responds with a statement about cognitive processing. An empathic response that expresses what the child has said may be as follows:

> Counsellor: It seems that what you're saying is that your acne has affected the way that you feel on several levels. It affects how you feel at school, at home and even with your relationship with your boyfriend. It sounds like you feel that you don't even like who you are any more.

This response captures what the child has said. The response from the counsellor and the child are almost interchangeable. The counsellor expresses the same feelings as the child though they do not help the child go deeper into her own experience. An even more empathic response would be something like:

> Counsellor: I guess what you're saying is that when the acne gets worse it affects everything you do and everything you are. It's like there is not way to control it. It takes over, affecting how others see you and how you see yourself.

This statement not only reflects what the child has just said, but also identifies feelings that the child has not verbalised. This statement expresses meaning and emotion at a deeper level than the child was able to express herself.

A 'level 5 response' is considered to be the most empathic response that a counsellor can make to a child. In this case it might be along the lines of the following:

> Counsellor: It sounds like what you're saying is that when the acne flares up, that it's as if you have no control over parts of your life. It's as if when it gets worse there is nothing you can do, it affects so many parts of your life at the same time that it just seems impossible to cope sometimes. It seems that what you're saying is when the acne gets worse, you don't only hate the way it looks, but that you don't like who you become.

A response such as this adds to what the child has said by expressing feelings that the child was unable to express herself, and also by helping the child to explore her experience at a deeper level.

Summarising

Summarising is a useful technique when counselling young people. It helps the counsellor to draw together what has been said and reflect to the child 'the bigger picture' of what has happened during the session. It is important to note that, as is the case with empathic responses, the counsellor should be careful not to be too interpretive or to add too much new material to what is being said. Summarising is about pulling together information to see how it fits, or does not fit, as the case may be (see Box 5.4).

Box 5.4

Summarising

- Drawing together feelings and observations made by the child.
- Presenting the child with a 'bigger picture' of what has been covered so far.
- Making salient any inconsistencies between feelings and observations that the child has made and therefore allowing him/her to explore this.
- Helping the child to look at what has been covered in a more complete way and allowing him/her to make connections with regard to what has been said.

Feelings that you are not doing enough

A common feeling amongst all counsellors, especially those who have only limited experience, is that they may not be doing enough to help the child. The effect of the core skills described above on the child and the counselling session should not be underestimated. Although other skills are important (and these are covered in the remaining chapters), they may not be well received by the child if the core conditions are ignored. Take for example the way that the empathic responses above were worded: '*It seems like … I guess … You appear to be saying…*' Each of these prefaces may appear to be merely reflecting what the child has just said. But if delivered sensitively, these responses also convey respect to the child. Although you may know more about counselling than the children you see, they are the ones who know about their own experience. Empathy creates a climate in which the children feel free to talk to or disagree with what the counsellor says and also empowers them to make changes in their lives which best suit their own circumstances. Most of all, creating a context of empathy encourages the child actively to participate in the counselling process.

Although the techniques described above are useful, it is appropriate that some children and problems will require practical, concrete coping tools and interventions. A more directive approach to counselling can also be included where children can be prompted actively to participate in behavioural and cognitive tasks that will help them to cope with particular situations. A discussion of some of these techniques is outlined below.

Strategies for facilitating change

Identifying negative thoughts or cognitive distortions

The beliefs that children hold about their problem may influence how they cope with and adapt to it. Beliefs may be: 'I have done something bad to deserve this' or 'My life is now ruined', among many others. A common feature among people who feel depressed or anxious is that they have negative, and at times seemingly irrational, thoughts about their life. These perceptions are often the result of 'errors in processing' whereby experiences and interpretations are distorted (Beck, 1976). Such 'cognitive errors' include the following:

- *Elective abstraction* – attending only to negative aspects of experience, so that the problem becomes the defining feature of the child's outward appearance: 'It doesn't matter that people say that I have a nice body or pretty eyes; the only thing that I notice about myself is the eczema.'
- *Personalisation* – feeling responsible or upset about things that have nothing to do with oneself: 'Mummy and Daddy divorced because Daddy didn't want to live with me.'
- *Arbitrary inference* – reaching conclusions based on insufficient or inadequate evidence: 'The reason that he asked me to his party is because he feels sorry for me; there is no way that somebody who knows about my problems would want to invite me.'
- *All-or-nothing thinking* – thinking in extremes: 'If I can't get to the point where this is sorted out, then I'll never be happy.'

- *Generalisation* – exaggerating the effect of an unpleasant experience so that it affects every aspect of one's life, no matter how unrelated: 'My friend's sister runs away when I come into the room; everybody hates me.'
- *Catastrophising* – thinking of only the worst-case scenario and hugely exaggerating the effects of what might happen: 'If Daddy leaves then I will never see him again and he will forget about me and won't know who I am.'

It might be useful first to identify and then discuss these cognitive errors with the child and examine whether some of the conclusions that they have reached about their problem may be the result of these.

Use of questions in challenging thinking errors

One of the most useful ways to challenge negative or irrational thoughts is through questioning. Indeed, it is more effective to elicit rational thoughts through the use of questioning than to encourage the child to think of 'rational' alternatives. By so doing, the child is encouraged to think through alternatives to their beliefs or responses, rather than being told what to think.

The way that the question is asked is also important. 'Why' questions are usually hard to answer (e.g. 'Why do you disrupt classes?') and may lead to vague and usually short responses, such as: 'I'm not sure' or 'I don't know'. 'What' and 'How' questions are more useful, for example, asking: 'Why do you disrupt classes?' may not be as useful as asking: 'What do you hope to gain when you disrupt classes?'

Another useful questioning technique that helps to challenge negative thoughts are questions that try to get at the 'worst-case scenario' that the child anticipates. For example, a counsellor might ask a child who is worried about other people noticing his eczema: 'What is the worst thing that you could imagine if someone was to see the skin on your arms?'

Child:	That they would stare at me and wonder what was wrong with my skin.
Counsellor:	Well, let's assume that that's what would happen, in what way would that be such a terrible thing?
Child:	I don't know, I just hate the idea of people staring at me. It makes me feel uncomfortable, I never know what to do.
Counsellor:	Perhaps if we could work on some practical coping strategies together such as making eye contact with the person that is staring, or diverting your attention to something else, do you think that would be useful?
Child:	Yes, that's my main problem you see, I never know what to do. If I had a way to deal with it then I wouldn't get so anxious when I thought about it.

In some cases, the child is anxious about certain situations or events but does not understand why. By asking questions relating to 'worst-case scenarios' the child is challenged to examine his own thoughts and apprehensions and these can then be discussed during the session.

Thought monitoring

As mentioned earlier, it is not situations in and of themselves that are always stressful or depressing, but rather the perception that we have of them. If we learn first to identify negative or erroneous thoughts and then to challenge them, we can influence our interpretation of emotional reactions to various situations. Helping the child to become more aware of his thoughts can be achieved by asking him record when he is feeling emotionally upset and the problem situations in which he finds himself. The counsellor first discusses with the child the importance of attributions in how we feel and react in different situations. During the session, the counsellor might also discuss examples of negative or erroneous thinking that the child has displayed during the session, and alternative rational responses to these thoughts. For example:

Child:　　　I don't want to go to school. I think all the children and teachers at the school will notice my eczema and won't want to talk to me.

Counsellor:　That sounds like quite an extreme reaction you are expecting. I wonder why you're expecting this to happen. Has it ever happened before?

Child:　　　Well no, but I just feel that when they look at me, they won't like me because of the way I look.

Counsellor:　I see. Is that the way you usually decide if you like someone or not, or whether to talk to them?

Child:　　　Of course not. But appearance is important.

Counsellor:　Sure it's important, but so are a lot of other things including how friendly you are and how you relate to other people. Since you said that you don't make judgements about liking people based on the way they look, is it likely that others do the same?

Child:　　　I guess so.

Counsellor:　Also consider this, in all your past experience this extreme reaction you're expecting has never happened to you, right? Then how can you be certain that people will dislike you because of the appearance of your skin?

Child:　　　I suppose so. Maybe I was exaggerating what I thought they would think. No one has ever said, 'I hate you because of your skin.'

Once the child is clear about the process, the counsellor can introduce the concept of monitoring thoughts for homework. The child in this case was asked to complete a pre-printed thought monitoring sheet (see Table 5.1) and return with it to the next counselling session for discussion. It is important that the child fill in the sheet at the time that they are experiencing the emotional upset or as close to it as possible, so that they are more likely to recall accurately their negative thoughts.

It should be noted that some conditions may be more stigmatising in certain cultures than others, and therefore what may seem to be an irrational or negative belief from the child's perspective may actually be valid within their specific

TABLE 5.1 *Thought monitoring*

Actual or anticipated situation	Negative thoughts	Emotion/ behaviour	Alternative thoughts	Emotion/ behaviour
I went to the swimming pool and was worried that people would be staring at my arms and legs.	I feel ugly because of my skin and I know that other people will look at my skin and won't like it.	Miserable, sad, stressed, I don't want to be here.	There are lots of people at the swimming pool. They probably won't even notice me. Just because I have bad skin it doesn't mean I'm a bad person.	This made me feel a bit more relaxed. I was still worried but I didn't see any people staring at me.

context. It is important, therefore, that counsellors be aware of such cultural differences and take account of these in their discussions with the child.

Thought blocking

Thought blocking is a technique commonly used with children suffering from obsessive disorders. It provides a means of dismissing intrusive thoughts and thus reducing their duration. In the example of eczema, recurring thoughts regarding one's appearance are common. Even though these are not likely to be classified as obsessive, the child nevertheless may often find himself becoming overly anxious regarding how others are reacting to the way that they look and may engage in checking behaviours to see whether their condition has changed. In order to help the child cope with these recurring thoughts and reduce the frequency of checking behaviours, a technique known as thought blocking may be used.

The child is initially asked to describe the different recurring thoughts that he has had and when and where these tend to take place. The counsellor then explains to the child that they will describe one of these situations and that as soon as he begins having the recurring thought to put a hand up. As soon as the child has raised the hand, the counsellor shouts, 'Stop!' The child is then asked what happened to the thought, which should have disappeared. This is then repeated with different thoughts that the child has identified until he feels ready to try 'stopping' thoughts on their own. When in public it will of course be difficult for children to shout 'Stop!' out loud, so as an alternative they may opt to wear a rubber band around their wrist and to snap it sharply when they begin to feel the recurring thought coming on. Thought stopping should be practised as homework and any difficulties identified and reported back to the counsellor (Hawton et al., 1994).

Distraction

Another means of controlling anxiety due to negative thoughts is through the use of distraction. This technique is often used when the child finds himself becoming anxious or distressed in a particular situation. If, for example, they begin to feel anxious while on a bus because of the crowds of people, then distraction may

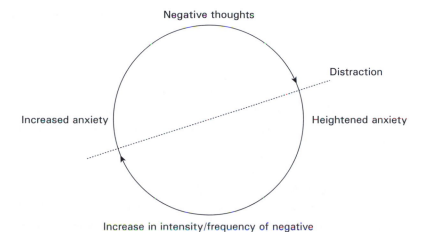

FIGURE 5.1   *Vicious cycle set up by negative thoughts and how distraction can help break the cycle*

be used as a means to help them divert their attention from the anxiety-provoking thoughts or stimulus. There are several ways that this can be done. First, the child may be asked to focus their attention on a neutral event or object. They may be asked to count how many people on the bus are wearing blue sweaters or how many cars overtook them in the last five minutes. Second, mental exercises may be used, such as reciting the alphabet backwards or counting to one hundred in multiples of five.

Finally, another useful technique involves asking the child to recall in detail a pleasant memory or fantasy that they may have. This may be a recent holiday or dreaming what they would do if they won the lottery. Through the use of distraction, the child is then able to control his anxiety and this in turn prevents a vicious cycle from building up whereby negative thoughts make the child anxious and this anxiety further exacerbates negative thoughts.

Relaxation

Relaxation is a useful way to help children prepare for anxiety-provoking situations or to cope with stressful social predicaments. Relaxation can be used on its own as a means to reduce anxiety and tension, or can be paired up with imagery to help the child prepare for potentially difficult or stressful situations. There are various different techniques that can be used. The series of relaxation steps is as follows:

1   The initial stage of this training involves teaching the child to distinguish between tension and relaxation that they feel in their bodies. Through this, they learn to become aware of when they are feeling tense. The child is asked

to sit in a comfortable chair while the counsellor models how muscles can be tensed and relaxed by clenching and relaxing their jaw, tensing and releasing their fists, etc.

2 The child is asked to close his eyes and the counsellor begins to take the child through the various muscle groups, beginning from the face and moving down to the shoulders, neck, arms, torso and legs.

3 The child is asked to maintain the tension for approximately five seconds and then relax the same muscle group for approximately ten seconds. This is done for each muscle group.

4 After finishing all the muscle groups the child is asked to rate how relaxed he or she feels from a scale from one to a hundred.

5 The counsellor checks whether or not the child has had any problems with a particular muscle group and if so he or she is helped to work through this.

6 The child is asked to practise progressive relaxation daily and keep a record of the time taken to relax and the extent of relaxation achieved on a scale of one to a hundred.

As the child becomes more accustomed to using progressive relaxation, the time taken to relax can be reduced by omitting the tension exercises.

Using imagery to cope with anxiety-provoking situations

The concept of employing imagery to help people cope with anxiety relating to their problem is based on the principle that if you can prepare for a situation which you predict will be stressful or anxiety provoking, you should be able to cope better with it. A useful technique is to help the child visualise the feared situation while in a relaxed state. If the child can feel relaxed while imaging the feared stimulus, then it is more likely that they will be relaxed when the actual situation occurs. Below are some important steps in helping children prepare for anxiety-provoking situations.

- Establish with the child what exactly the feared stimulus is and what about it makes them feel anxious. By establishing the exact nature of the child's anxiety, you will be able to tailor the visualisation exercise to address this.
- Help the child to relax by asking them to sit comfortably, and to become aware of any tension they are feeling in their muscles (see section above on relaxation). Speak slowly and clearly and make sure there are no interruptions while this is happening.
- While the child is in the relaxed state, ask him or her to imagine the feared scenario, giving as much detail as possible regarding the location and what is happening. For example, ask them to describe where they will be, who will be there, what they will be wearing, etc. Throughout your description, check how anxious or nervous they feel, reassuring them that they are safe and reminding them to breathe steadily and relax.
- Help the child to visualise how he might react to the feared stimulus/situation and give realistic suggestions as to what might happen. For example, the child might be worried about getting lost. Give suggestions about possible actions

they can take if this happens and suggest the likely outcome to these actions. Keep monitoring the child's state of relaxation and breathing.

- Finally, end the visualisation by asking the child how they feel and check with them what the visualisation exercise felt like and whether they thought it was useful. They may also be given an 'intrusive thought' to repeat to themselves outside the session to maintain the effects. This could be in the form of a mantra such as: it may feel stressful and this may be uncomfortable but stress of this kind is not dangerous.

Once the child feels that he is comfortable with the visualisation exercise, you can begin discussing the possibility of trying out an exercise between sessions.

Homework

Homework tasks can prove a useful tool in counselling. For most children, home-work may be a term that has negative connotations. It is important to take care to explain what is implied by 'homework' in counselling. Tasks should be devised to enable the child to practise and master counselling interventions (e.g. counter-ing negative thoughts, relaxation). They may be asked to keep a diary of their thoughts regarding their condition, or to practise relaxation techniques and report back on their progress in subsequent sessions. It is important that the homework task is discussed and agreed upon by both child and counsellor. This way, the task is more likely to be relevant to the child's problems and therefore the child is more likely to be motivated to carry it out.

Once the homework task has been decided upon, the counsellor needs to clarify what should be done, where and how many times. It is also important that the counsellor ensures that the child understands the reason behind doing the homework. Finally, the counsellor assesses the child's commitment to carrying out the homework. The counsellor might ask, for example, whether or not the child can foresee any difficulties in carrying out the task. If problems are identi-fied the counsellor can address them with the child or focus on them more in the counselling sessions before assigning them as homework tasks.

Maintaining changes derived from counselling sessions

Towards the end of counselling, the child might express concern about how he will cope having left the safety of the counselling environment and may feel uneasy about how well they will be able to put the benefits of counselling into practice and to maintain them. These concerns should not be dismissed. Endings in counselling have the potential either to reinforce change or undo the gains achieved. It is important to reassure the child that it is 'normal' or 'expected' that there will be some level of relapse in some situations. This may be because their confidence slips or they become anxious that they do not have the safety of the counselling sessions in which to talk about their concerns. Predicting some relapse and providing some reassurance about this is an important and helpful therapeutic intervention in itself. Some additional strategies for helping the child end counselling are outlined below:

- Prepare the child for the end of counselling by a reminder in the last few sessions leading up to the end that the course of counselling will be drawing to a finish.
- Remind the child of the gains made during the course of counselling. If they have kept a diary, look over it together comparing how they felt at the beginning of counselling and how they feel now.
- Discuss with the child the importance of continuing to carry out the challenges to negative thoughts, relaxation techniques or whatever else the child found useful during counselling.
- Remind the child that although you spent time together working on the problem, the majority of the time the child worked at it alone and therefore the child is the most important part of the counselling process.

Conclusion

This chapter has provided an understanding of the central issues and strategies involved in counselling. The skills that were described highlighted the importance of the counselling relationship and how, through the application of empathy, genuineness and unconditional positive regard, children can make positive progress in resolving or coming to terms with their problems. The idea that empathy is more than mere reflection was emphasised and examples of different levels and types of empathic responses were given. We also described how cognitive behavioural techniques can be applied in this setting to achieve specific goals with the child. The remaining chapters explore these and further therapeutic concepts in greater detail.

6 Brief and Positive Counselling Interventions with Pupils

Doing therapy in a school setting is demanding. It can even seem tedious at times. Working with large numbers of pupils, similar in age, often dressed in a similar fashion, can tax the most alert, resourceful, diligent and committed counsellor. It requires effort on the part of the counsellor to remain focused. To retain the ability to approach each new encounter with the openness and freshness it deserves is challenging.

Research findings can help the counsellor to stay on track. Modern counselling research indicates that one of the critical components which contributes to a successful outcome is the degree to which the client participates in the process of counselling (Miller et al., 1997). It becomes a useful exercise then for the busy school counsellor to consider what she says and does that engages the pupil into the process of counselling. The counsellor needs to be able to convey to the client that he is understood. However, counselling has to be more than this to be helpful to the client. The client needs to experience 'newness' in some shape or form, in order for him to move on from his 'stuck' position.

Combining a stance of active listening and real concern to the systemic notion of curiosity can progress the counselling process. The school counsellor needs to reposition herself alongside the pupil. What this means in real terms is that the counsellor adopts a collaborative approach towards working with the pupil. She needs to utilise her repertoire of skills to elicit the pupil's opinion and to engage and encourage him actively to participate in the counselling conversation. This is a radical shift from the traditional stance of the counsellor as expert, out ahead of the client, with the solution to the problem already worked out. It means approaching the pupil with an attitude that actively seeks his help. 'Help me understand ...' is a phrase that could usefully prefix almost every intervention made by the counsellor.

Assuming a genuinely curious stance is not optional in initiating a productive and potentially useful working relationship with the schoolchild. The counsellor is in need of the pupil's co-operation so that the real issues can be identified and addressed. Only the pupil himself can know what is actually going on in the current situation. Twelve-year-old Mark was sent to the school counsellor for punching Joe at school break. However, only Mark knew that Joe and his friends lay in wait for him each day outside the school gates where they assaulted and taunted him. The real issue is that Mark was being bullied. The punching behaviour was an expression of Mark's need to assert and defend himself. Joe and his friends had told Mark that if he told anyone what was actually going on, he would be 'done for'. Mark did not understand the meaning of the words 'done for'. He only knew that these words filled him with dread. He was petrified.

It takes skill, sensitivity and a deftness of approach on the part of the counsellor to cut through Mark's fear so that he feels able to say what is really going on for him. Working thus keeps the counsellor on her toes and mitigates against any sense of complacency or tedium. It is of course rewarding and satisfying if Mark's story is elicited and appropriate help and support are provided.

The remainder of this chapter consists of a variety of suggestions firmly grounded on the theoretical principles described in this book that inform a certain approach to counselling the schoolchild. The suggestions are not intended to be either an exhaustive, novel or comprehensive list of techniques, but rather an attempt to illustrate an operational, co-operative, brief and positive way of working with the schoolchild. The interventions described loosely follow the structure and sequence of a counselling session, to aid the reader's understanding of not only how to implement the interventions, but also when and at what point they might be utilised. The suggestions that are made may serve as prompts for the school counsellor to work creatively to develop her practice in her own unique setting.

Approaching the first encounter

It is useful to begin working with school-aged children with an attitude that radiates an openness and friendliness. To smile is helpful. Young people and children tend to smile easily and frequently respond well if they are smiled at. It is equally important for the counsellor to convey the sense that she is in charge of the process. This is a business-like encounter. Indeed everything the counsellor says and does should convey the message to the pupil that this is a safe place for him to be. The early outlining of the parameters of the counselling process in terms of length and spacing of sessions and the structure of the process can create a sense of safety and stability for the schoolchild who may be feeling that things are getting out of control.

One way of explaining the limits of confidentiality is as follows: 'If you were to tell me that once you leave this room you are planning to murder the first teacher you meet, then I wouldn't be able to keep this information to myself.' Such an approach rarely fails to elicit a smile from the child. It can help both to relax and engage the young person. At the same time it is putting firm boundaries in place.

In a school setting, pupils are frequently sent to the school counsellor having committed some misdemeanour. They may arrive at the school counsellor's room feeling judged or censured. The school counsellor may be perceived by the pupil as an authority figure. The fear may exist for the pupil that even further criticism or judgement will ensue in this encounter. Such negative feelings need to be addressed early in the meeting.

> Whose idea was it that you come and talk to me?

Such a question is an example of simple and direct communication. It is respectful of the pupil. Pupils usually have no difficulty in giving the required information. It can be quickly followed with:

> What did you think of the idea of coming to talk to me?

This question may take the young person by surprise as it may be his first experience of having his opinion sought. If the response to this question suggests that the pupil has been sent to the counsellor and the pupil himself would rather not be there, a suggested way to proceed might be:

> You know you don't have to talk to me. We could sit here together and you could do your homework. Alternatively, you and I could try and work out together what you need to do to get Mr Ryan off your back/show Mr Ryan that you are making an effort.

A suggestion such as this epitomises the collaborative approach. It is an attempt to connect with the person of the pupil. It ignores any negative labelling or description. It also has a lightness of touch that may appeal to the young person.

> How long do you think this may take?

To suggest that this might be just a one-off conversation might come as a relief to the reluctant child and help to lighten the atmosphere. Another suggestion to engage the pupil might be:

> You know I'm not 15 anymore. I need your help to understand better how things feel for you.

This is a very upfront and honest approach. Its simplicity and directness may disarm the youngster and co-opt him into the process. It sets the tone for working collaboratively with the young person. A questioning approach is inherent to collaborative working. A question of itself is invitational in nature and so elicits the pupil's response.

Uncovering strengths and resources by adopting a positive attitude

Having given the child sufficient time and space to express his story of distress, the counsellor might reflect:

> How have you managed to put up with all that's been happening to you? Have you always been so brave?

Young people are especially sensitive to adverse labelling and criticism. Pupils in schools frequently come to the counsellor burdened by negative descriptions of themselves as already stated, whether these are from professionals, peers, family members or even themselves. To be addressed positively and directly as illustrated above may come as a complete surprise to the young person. It may even take his breath away. A common answer to such a question is: 'I don't know. I haven't thought about it.' This may be accompanied by a look of puzzlement. Such an apparently non-committal response may be full of significance. It may represent a fundamental shift in premise. It can mean that the young person has begun to consider himself differently. If he has not outrightly dismissed the new positive description of himself, it means that he has at least been stopped in his tracks. He has taken the first small step in altering his own perception of himself to take on board an alternative one. Connecting at such a significant level is at the heart of the counselling process. Offering a direct compliment can be a powerful therapeutic intervention in itself:

> Gosh, you are really brave. Are you aware of that?
> Has anyone else said that to you before?

Such a positive and direct compliment can go a long way to encourage a new way of thinking in the child. Questions or statements about skills, competence and positive qualities can set the counselling conversation on a very different track to that of a conversation that confines itself only to a discussion of the child's pain or despair. Children often do not have as many choices about the circumstances of their lives as adults. Bravery, courage, endurance can frequently be found, if looked for. Such compliments, as illustrated, can be delivered genuinely. To engage a child in a conversation about his positive qualities and resourcefulness may count for much more than might be thought. Such conversations can create space and give definition to such skills and resources that may be all that the pupil has to draw on to carry him through in the taxing circumstances in which he finds himself.

Much depends on the counsellor's own ability to recognise not only the distress and pain in the child in front of her, but also how that child has managed to live through and endure; to find courage and resilience to survive. The ability to be able to notice and assign space and definition to such qualities is essential. Skills developed in the child in the face of adversity may include the ability to:

- judge true friendship, trust and loyalty
- survive isolation and distress
- endure feeling different
- have values different from one's peers.

These qualities may well go unnoticed unless deliberately looked for and acknowledged. It takes effort on the part of the counsellor to do just that.

Fifteen-year-old Gerard had been referred to the school counsellor for failure to attend school by his Head of Year. Gerard, like Mark already mentioned, had been subjected to daily cruel bullying by a group of his peers. Gerard could no longer face coming into school on a number of days each week. Gerard recounted to the counsellor how he had previously attempted to inform his form tutor about what was going on. His tutor had made Gerard's story public to the class in an attempt to help. As a result, Gerard had had his head pushed into the toilet bowl with the toilet flushed as a punishment by his peers. Gerard was getting more desperate by the day. He lived alone with his father. They were now constantly arguing as Gerard's father felt he could no longer trust him. Gerard had not revealed the extent of his suffering to his father as he did not want to distress him. Having heard his story of pain, the counsellor merely said to Gerard:

> How have you managed to drag yourself out of bed and into school on the days that you have?

Such a question reflects empathy at a profound level. Gerard's suffering is implicitly acknowledged. In referring to Gerard's ability to drag himself out of bed, the message was given that he is in control of his sadness. He is greater than the pain that drags him down. Gerard's response to this question was to burst into uncontrollable sobbing. With some prompting from the counsellor, Gerard continued his story. It began to emerge that the bullying he was subjected to had begun the previous summer term following a particular incident. Gerard had refused to participate in a group attack on a younger pupil new to the school. Even though this action was considered to be part of the ritual initiation of all new pupils to the school, Gerard found he did not have the heart to be involved. Subsequently Gerard began to see his peers in a different light. He gradually ceased his association with them. Soon after, Gerard himself had become the subject of bullying. The counsellor asked Gerard:

> Could it be that your friends felt judged and rejected by you?
> Could it be that your decision to distance yourself from your peers began this whole process?

Gerard looked startled. He thoughtfully exclaimed:

> You know I've never thought about it like that, but it is true! I rejected them before they turned on me.

Gerard continued to be taunted by his peers for some time after this counselling session. However, the bullying gradually ceased and no external help was initiated. Gerard had begun to behave differently towards the other pupils. He had lost his fear of them. He began to look them in the eye. His behaviour indicated to them that they were no longer able to upset him. He had begun to assume mastery in the situation. He was now regaining control in his life once again. The turning point had come for him in the first counselling session when he realised it was his decision and not that of his peers which had initiated the process of bullying. Thinking thus made Gerard feel that he had more control in the situation than he had previously understood. This new way of thinking made a big difference.

Creating a sense of movement

Questioning the pupil's fixity of thought

It is normal for a child to catastrophise. Children often do not have sufficient life experience to see beyond the most recent censure by a parent or teacher, rejection by peers, or lack of success in their favoured subject. Such moments can catapult the young person into such a subjective experience of distress that the risk of self-harm or suicide cannot be ignored by the counsellor. On a lighter note, absolute terminology can characterise a young person's conversation frequently. 'I have no friends', 'They never let me play', 'I'm never chosen', 'The teacher never asks me a question.' Such words as 'never' and 'always' can be usefully addressed by the counsellor. A series of well-chosen questions can help to reflect on what is being conveyed.

> You say the teacher never asks you a question? Help me understand what you're saying: you mean that from the time you began in this class the teacher has never asked you a single question? … Let me be clear about this, she has asked every other kid in the class a question at sometime or other? … She doesn't even ask if you are present as she calls the register each day?

This very direct questioning, which is entirely uncritical, can shake the pupil's certainty of thought about his experience. It may help him to begin to think afresh about the current situation. If a sense of the ridiculous is evoked, this in itself can be a positive sign that absolute certainty is loosening its grip on the pupil's judgement. Space may then be created to allow the possibility of another perspective or another explanation to emerge. Again, it is not uncommon for a teenager who is feeling unfairly treated by his parents or teachers to preface his arguments with statements such as the following: 'All my friends are allowed out for as long as they like at the weekends.' It can be a useful exercise to elicit the actual meaning of the word 'all'. Not infrequently, it may be uncovered that 'all' equates with 'Matthew' who appears to be enjoying more parental leniency than any other individual in the peer group. Thoughtful silence on the part of the young person can often be the response to such logical inquisitiveness. Silence may signify a difference in thinking, especially if up to this point the teenager's most notable characteristic has been vociferousness. When any indication of movement in fixity of approach is encountered, it can be a sign that change is happening in the current situation.

Looking ahead

The objective of the well-documented miracle question (de Shazer, 1985) is to create some sense of movement in the current stuck situation. Pupils can be asked to describe their preferred scenario for the future. Silence can often be the first response to this proposition. Such silence may not denote an unwillingness to complete the task, but signifies rather the struggle to imagine things that have not yet happened – life without the current distress. The exercise is worth pursuing.

Such a task is a direct challenge to the young person's resourcefulness. A pupil suffering family distress such as parents' divorce may be encouraged to look to the future and imagine, for example, what university life might be like. This may be sufficient in itself to:

- encourage him through the current painful circumstances;
- prioritise what is important;
- help elicit sufficient endurance to keep him on track in the face of rigorous academic demands.

Having discussed in some detail a young person's preferred future, questions that might be useful to ask are as follows:

Which bit of the miracle that you have described is already present in your life?

or

Is there any bit of the miracle that you could make happen right now?

A surprising answer to one of the above questions came from a 17-year-old boy who was discovering his homosexual orientation. He told the counsellor that it was his secret life that currently kept him going through the agony of his parents' acrimonious divorce. He said that he looked forward to further joyful exploration of his sexuality when he would be living independently at university. Having a conversation about the future can give it a reality that instils hope in the present distress.

Goal identification

Goals need to be realistic, specific, jointly negotiated, measurable and identified as early as possible in the counselling encounter. Goal identification creates a focus for the work. It keeps the end in view right from the beginning. It also keeps counselling relevant and brief. The goals of any counselling encounter may not be apparent at the beginning of the first session. They can be identified only by working closely with the pupil.

Fifteen-year-old Thomas had been referred to the school counsellor for poor academic performance. Thomas was a bright pupil. In the past, his academic performance had been outstanding. Thomas's reward for such achievement by his peers was to have the word 'swot' scratched on his arm with a compass tip. He had also been excluded from all peer group activity. Thomas was very unhappy. He had reduced his academic output in order to survive in the situation. However, he had not anticipated being dropped from the school football team, which was what happened when his academic performance plummeted. This was a bitter blow for him. When Thomas came for counselling he was quite clear about his own goal. It was to be reinstated on the football team. Such a goal was clear, specific, measurable and desirable. It was a clear aim in the midst of a complex situation. It would require much effort on his part sufficiently to raise his academic standard. It would also involve liaison work with his teachers so that a measure of protection could be put in place for him and the bullying behaviour addressed and stopped. The counsellor on her own could never have formulated such a goal. Goals have to be jointly negotiated between pupil and counsellor for them to be relevant in the situation and desired by the pupil. The pupil has to want to achieve the goal as considerable effort is required in order to achieve it. Effort in this regard does not appear to be a deterrent.

Measuring change

One of the most effective ways of recognising and endorsing change is by measuring it. Indeed, the idea of measurement both during a counselling session and between sessions is central to many modern models of therapy. This is particularly true of the cognitive-behavioural approach. One simple and practical way of doing this is by using a simple linear ten-point scale. Creativity and imagination can be utilised to make the activity age appropriate. Point zero can represent the low point – distress at its most severe; performance or behaviour at its least desirable. Point ten can represent the pupil's preferred scenario. When the pupil is invited to self-assess, the scale becomes an instrument that encourages pupil participation and self-reflection. Even very young pupils can be actively engaged in such an exercise. The scale can be pictorially represented, for example, with a line of sad or happy faces.

   Such activity can be carried out at any point in the counselling relationship. If used at the beginning of the first encounter, it is a simple way of clarifying the ground to be covered in a specific, clear, manageable and measured way. Ten pieces of course work remain to be written before Thomas gets near to reselection for the football team. A point on the scale can represent each piece of coursework. Progress already made towards the desired outcome can be clearly measured. Thomas had in fact already completed two pieces of coursework prior to the first counselling session, represented by two points on the scale. The counsellor might go on to ask Thomas:

   How did you manage to get yourself into position two, Thomas?

Any point on the scale can be thought of as a positive achievement. Thomas may need some prompting to work out how he managed to discipline himself into getting the paper and pen out, marshalling the research and producing two pieces of coursework. The thought process and behaviour that led Thomas to perform this new behaviour can be elicited and built upon. Such questioning can foster hope and encourage a sense of mastery in the situation. Scaling questions can be used to create a focus in the work. They can be used even at serious moments in counselling. In the assessment of risk of self-harm or suicidal intent the following approach might be utilised:

Point zero on the scale may be used to represent the point in which you most feel like harming yourself. Where would you place yourself today?

Answers to such questions can make the objectives of counselling specific, relevant and clear. Seventeen-year-old Alice, to whom the above question was directed, placed herself at point six on the scale. Such self-assessment can be scrutinised further, but the indication is that counselling may continue. Had Alice placed herself at point two or lower on the scale, emergency measures to ensure her safety would be prioritised and counselling suspended until a more appropriate time.

The use of scaling questions can help keep the work on track from session to session:

Counsellor: Last session you described yourself as being on point six of the scale. Where would you place yourself today?
Pupil: Point five.
Counsellor: What's happened to make you lose ground?

Such questions help to make the work specific. No time is wasted in identifying a focus for the session. Scaling questions can also be very useful at the end of the counselling sessions in order to map out progress made.

Conclusion

This chapter has attempted to illustrate the application of theoretical principles underpinning this book to the actual practice of counselling in a school session. The objective has not been to carry out this task in an ordered and systematic fashion, but rather to give a flavour of the vibrant, living process of working as a counsellor in the often complex and demanding day-to-day life of a school. Hopefully in their application to day-to-day life in a school, there is a freshness of approach that will prove beneficial.

Our understanding of counselling is based on the very traditional view that the heart of the counselling process is about forging a positive relationship. Modern theoretical ideas have helped our understanding of how the therapeutic relationship may be extended in order to be more useful for pupils. Essentially our understanding rests on the belief that for a relationship to happen the active contribution of both participants is required. In our experience, to adopt a positive, respectful and upfront attitude is the best way to elicit the pupil's full participation in the process of counselling.

The illustrations in this chapter have been thoughtfully selected to demonstrate that the pupil's participation is not optional, but rather an essential component to working effectively and efficiently. The modern counsellor can no longer operate on the basis that she knows best. To work as creatively as required by the approach described in this book makes demands on the counsellor's own understanding and skill. She needs to be able to develop her capacity to listen and to see beyond the current situation; to be able to notice and acknowledge competence skills and resources in the pupil that are not obvious to him, but will enable him to take on the business of his life in a more robust, resilient and joyful way, once he realises they exist. Lest this task feels too great, it is important to state that it is not the counsellor's responsibility to always get things right. The objective of counselling is more modest than this. It can be simply described in terms of getting the pupil back on track and able to access his own creativity and strengths about what the next step is in any given situation.

Counsellors only have words in their toolkit to help them in their work of counselling. Modern theoretical ideas have extended our understanding of the role of language in counselling. The process of counselling as illustrated by the case examples in this chapter all happens in words. The pupil's understanding of himself can be changed when different words are selected to describe the situation in which he finds himself. It is not an exaggeration to say that the words with which we choose to describe ourselves contribute to making us who we are.

When pupils come to the school counsellor, as mentioned already, they are frequently burdened by negative descriptions of themselves. 'I'm no good', 'I'm not able' or 'I'm bad' are not uncommon descriptions elicited in the first encounter. A question that might usefully be addressed to the pupil and not made explicit so far in this chapter might be as follows: 'How come you chose to understand yourself only in this way?' (Strong, 2000: 25–42). Such a question could be seen as an apt summary of the approach described. As a question it invites collaboration and also implies possibility. The suggestion is that there are other possible understandings and descriptions available. It challenges the pupil. It creates focus by attempting to get directly to the point. It is collaborative and positive in its orientation. It can also herald the end of the therapeutic encounter if it is taken on board by the schoolchild to whom it is addressed.

7 Legal and Confidentiality Issues in Counselling Children

When counselling children, legal issues should be at the forefront of the counsellor's mind and practice. After all, the counsellor has a duty to ensure that the child's needs are understood and acknowledged above all else that may be transacted in and around sessions. Much has been written about counselling and therapy with children with an emphasis on the legal issues. It is not within the scope of this book to provide an exhaustive account of the specific legalities of certain situations. In this chapter, we provide an overview of the key issues that counsellors need to address when working with children in a school setting.

The Children Act 1989

While the provision of children's rights has been enshrined in law for most of the twentieth century, the major refinements have been to the implementation of these rights. For example, the 1987 Cleveland Report criticised the breakdown in liaison between different agencies supposedly acting on behalf of 120 children in Cleveland who were alleged to have been physically or sexually abused. These children were taken into care. However, the police and media appeared to have different views as to the causes of the breakdown from the medical practitioners and social workers charged with investigating and assessing the allegations. The question posed in the report was whether the children's interests were being assigned priority and whether they were in any way involved in the decision-making processes around their care. This report helped shape the Children Act 1989 which was implemented in 1991 (Department of Health 1991). The Act promotes the involvement of children in decisions that affect them; their interests and needs are seen to be paramount.

The Victorian belief that children were possessions has been totally reversed. Parents are now seen to have responsibilities and this replaces the concept of 'parental rights'. Children can apply to court for support and protection. Counsellors have to acknowledge these rights and seek to promote them. A further theme associated with the Children Act is a clear commitment to multidisciplinary teamwork among professional carers. Courts are required to take into account a range of factors before making decisions about the protection and care of a child which include:

- the wishes and feelings of the child;
- his emotional, physical and educational needs;

- his age, gender and harm or risk of suffering;
- the capabilities and means of the parents, among others;
- any harm that the child may have suffered or be at risk from suffering;
- the possible effects on the child of a change in circumstance.

The underlying tenet of the Children Act is that children are better off being brought up in their own families. However, in cases where this cannot or, in the eyes of the court, should not take place, the emphasis is on acting quickly to resettle the child in an environment that is considered more beneficial to him. To this end, Section 8 of the Act outlines four different orders that may be dealt with by the court:

1 Residence orders – those which determine where the child is to live.
2 Contact orders – those which decide who should be allowed access to the child.
3 Prohibited steps orders – those which seek to forbid the application of parental care.
4 Specific issue orders – those which enable parents to submit a specific question to the court.

The Act also endeavours to put the responsibility for child welfare on local authorities. Section 17 declares that they 'have a duty to safeguard and promote the welfare of children who are in need within their area and to promote the upbringing of such children by their families, by providing a range and level of services appropriate to those children's needs'. The local authority should provide support in the welfare of a particular child if:

- he is unlikely to achieve or maintain or have the opportunity of achieving or maintaining a reasonable standard of health or development without the provision of service by a local authority;
- his health or development is likely to be significantly impaired or further impaired without the provision for him of such services;
- he is disabled.

In order to address the complex area of abuse, the Act recognises the area of 'significant harm', which includes psychological, emotional, physical and sexual abuse, and neglect. When contemplating the area of care or supervision orders, the court may proceed when it is confident of the following:

- The child concerned is suffering significant harm or is likely to suffer significant harm.
- The harm or likelihood of harm is attributable to the care given to the child or likely to be given to him if the order were not made, not being what it would be reasonable to expect a parent to give to him.
- The child is beyond parental control.

In addition to the above, the Act makes provision for an emergency protection order and an education supervision order. The former may be implemented in cases where there is a reasonable cause to believe that the child is likely to suffer significant harm and lasts for eight days (with a provision of extension for up to seven days). The latter lasts from one to three years and allocates a supervisor to the family, to help both child and parents. The supervisor is employed to advise the family and direct them towards the proper education of the child.

The Children Act 1989 builds on, and enhances, legislation put into place by the Education Reform Act 1988. In addition, almost every country in the world has ratified the United Nations Convention on the Rights of the Child 1989. Furthermore, most countries have laws which protect the welfare of children. However, this does not necessarily mean that children are automatically afforded the same rights and privileges as the adult population. To a large extent, it is the duty of those who work closely with children, for example, teachers, doctors, nurses, social welfare agencies, etc., to ensure that individual children's rights are upheld. Counsellors have a role to play in this. In view of the complex structure of the modern-day welfare and school systems, counsellors may need to develop links with other professionals and agencies in contact with the child, rather than acting in isolation. School counsellors cannot by law act in isolation. At the very least, they will be required to establish links with senior staff and the child protection teacher.

The ethical counsellor

A central dilemma confronts every counsellor who works with young people and children, particularly those who work in school settings. Most counsellors readily understand that effective therapeutic work requires a secure space and an under-taking to keep confidential that which is transacted in the sessions. Indeed, it may be the fact that these conversations take place away from the influence of parents, teachers and peers which is the core ingredient aiding progress and a positive out-come in counselling. However, there are limits to confidentiality when working with children, and all counsellors have legal obligations which may go against the tenor of confidentiality. Confidentiality in counselling is a privilege that is not without exception or limitation. The threat of harm (physical or psychological) to the child or others outweighs a guarantee of complete confidentiality. When working with adults there are clear and specific requirements for when any coun-sellor must breach confidentiality and disclose important information to others. This usually has to do with life-threatening situations where harm may come to either the client or others. When working with children, these requirements are not fundamentally different. Those disclosures which do not seem contentious to most counsellors are the threat of self-harm or suicide, homicide, parental neglect and sexual or physical abuse. The disclosure of underage sex and drug use is almost always controversial and requires careful consideration and discussion with one's supervisor.

TABLE 7.1   *Some signs of abuse or neglect*

Physical harm:

➢ Bruising
➢ Scarring
➢ Bandages/plasters
➢ Rubbing part of the body (e.g. genital area, arm)
➢ Cigarette burns
➢ Abstains from physical activities and resists using the changing room at school

Psychological abuse/harm:

➢ Apathy
➢ Withdrawal from social contact
➢ Loss of enthusiasm/energy
➢ Seeming to be preoccupied
➢ Tearful
➢ Misses school or is frequently late

Neglect:

➢ Socially withdrawn
➢ Untidy/unkempt
➢ Poor time-keeping
➢ Infrequent mention of parents/family life
➢ Possibly slow to develop emotionally
➢ Overly self-reliant

Signs of abuse or neglect

Apart from when the child explicitly discloses or draws attention to neglect or abuse, the counsellor may be one of the first in the school to detect the signs. It is obviously not possible to 'look inside' the child or for the counsellor to undertake a physical examination of the child. Therefore, she must rely on her intuition, questioning, observation and detection of patterns of behaviour. A guideline for the counsellor of 'When in doubt, consult!' is apt in this regard. The headteacher, named child protection teacher and school nurse should be the first point of contact. A list of some signs of abuse or neglect is described in Table 7.1, though this is by no means exhaustive.

The difference for the counsellor between working with adults and children may be whether to breach confidentiality without the child's knowledge and consent. Contrary to some popular wisdom, the counsellor's relationship with the client, and in particular with children, is not a privileged one in the same way as that between lawyer and client. There are four main constraints which govern counselling practice:

1   A code of professional conduct and ethical guidelines (e.g. the British Association for Counselling and Psychotherapy, and the British Psychological Society both have a code of conduct for practitioners, guidelines on confidentiality and the law and a system for investigating alleged

transgressions of professional conduct). Copies of the BACP Guidelines on Confidentiality: Counselling and the Law, and Confidentiality Guidelines for College Counsellors in Further Education and Sixth Form Colleges are contained in Appendices A and B.

2 Rules that regulate counselling practice in a given context or setting (e.g. the headteacher may choose to be informed about all cases where there may be the risk of physical or psychological harm to a pupil).

3 The law of the land, especially as it pertains to children (in the UK, for example, the Children Act 1989 specifically describes aspects of good practice relating to the care of children).

4 Common sense (promoting autonomy, justice, beneficence, non-malevolence). It goes without saying that everything that happens when counselling children must be for their direct benefit and in no way should a child be physically or psychologically harmed by counselling or the counsellor.

In seeking to uphold and promote the rights afforded to children in the Children Act 1989, counsellors may find themselves torn between supporting these rights on the one hand and intruding upon the child's family life on the other. The counsellor might also believe that greater harm could come to the child from reporting a case of abuse or harm, or they may be deterred by the complex and lengthy legal processes that follow. The counsellor has an additional duty to inform colleagues if there is a suspicion of abuse, even if this later proves to be unfounded.

Guidelines for child-centred practice

Below is a list of guidelines or hints which may help to mitigate against legal action being taken against a counsellor and to promote good practice when working with children:

- Be clear as to the nature of the relationship between counsellor and client. Is this a corridor chat, consultation with a parent, or counselling session with the child? Each scenario may carry with it different obligations for the counsellor.
- Negotiate a clear line of accountability to the headteacher and/or others within the school system. Discuss at an early stage what information is required by others in the school system and/or the parents. Where these may be at variance with the practices of the counsellor (including ethical guidelines), they need to be resolved before children are seen in counselling. Is specific feedback required to the headteacher, nurse, doctor, teacher, parent?
- A clear policy and protocol must be developed in which issues around confidentiality and privacy are unambiguously stated. Children must be told about the confidential nature of sessions at the start of counselling, but also informed about the limits to confidentiality and the reasons for this. This protocol should be made explicit and agreed upon by the counsellor and headteacher, as well as others who have a direct interest in the counselling service.

- If the counsellor is also a teacher, there is a danger of a blurring of professional boundaries. The teacher needs to consider how a dual relationship with the child can evolve without compromising the confidential nature of sessions.
- Keep clinical notes which record what has been discussed in sessions and perhaps even provide a transcript where contentious issues are raised. This enables the counsellor to prove and justify the exact details of any sessions that have been held.
- Practise defensively: always think about how a specific situation would be construed in a court of law. How would I be able to justify my actions and responses?
- Do not make assumptions about children's responses to life events that may trouble them. Ask directly about their feelings and responses. Record these in the notes.
- Always make a list of the key players who may be (or should be) also working with the child, e.g. social worker, doctor, etc. Document in your notes any consultations or discussions you have had with them.
- There is always a duty to protect the child. Where there is evidence of actual abuse or the suspicion of abuse, you are obliged to report this to the relevant authorities, even if there is a risk that this may damage the therapeutic relationship. The viability of the therapeutic relationship is never more important than the welfare of the child.
- If confidentiality needs to be broken, make notes about the reason(s) for this. Keep a record in the notes of any conversations with colleagues stating the name, date and time, and main points discussed.
- Ensure that in your role as counsellor you have access to a clinical supervisor with whom you can review your progress in cases and discuss relevant clinical dilemmas.

We have tried to convey to the reader that, unlike when counselling adults, the school-based counsellor has a duty to break confidentiality in certain situations and is also accountable (usually to the headteacher). There are obvious limits to and conditions placed on counselling practice in schools. These limits need not constrain practice and, if carefully conceived, a clear protocol may even enhance the service and help to promote the provision of effective counselling. The risk of not having thought through a policy and protocol is that the counsellor might be seen to collude with the abuse or threat of harm and would then be at risk of criticism, professional misconduct, or even be breaking the law.

The school counsellor must always be alert to the possibility of harm, abuse and neglect and discuss this with colleagues, where appropriate. Obviously, this also includes assessing whether a situation is immediately life threatening or whether the passage of time might ameliorate the effects of a more general problem. The involvement of parents must also be considered, though the primary duty is to ensure the care of the child. Inevitably, there will be occasions where confidentiality has to be broken. While this may undermine the integrity of the counselling relationship, thankfully these occasions are usually infrequent. Nonetheless, the counsellor is still acting within her professional role where such disclosure has to be made. In the majority of these difficult situations, the counsellor can do much to offset against some of the dynamics that may follow from the need to make disclosures outside the counselling relationship. This includes:

- prior discussion with the child;
- presenting a positive rationale to the child;
- commenting on the counsellor's legal duty to inform others;
- reaffirming the counsellor's commitment to creating a safe environment for the child;
- explaining that in the short term there may be some disruption and upset, but in the longer term, the aim is to ensure that things improve significantly for the child;
- reminding the child that the counselling relationship need not change and sessions can continue to be arranged.

Figure 7.1 may help you to focus on the key issues and decisions that need to be made in counselling when there is a suspicion or evidence that a child has been physically or psychologically harmed.

We have considered the importance of recognising and acting on child abuse, and the implications this has for the counsellor's professional practice. Inevitably, in these situations, the counsellor will be confronted with dynamics that surround secrecy and confidentiality.

Secrets and confidential information

There is a difference between secrets and confidential information. Secrecy means the keeping of information from others (unless it is a shared secret), while confidential information, in the context of school-based counselling, is a shared secret, perhaps within a subsystem of the school, such as between the counsellor and headteacher or school doctor. The extent to which a secret has been shared is not always easy to distinguish. When a secret is finally revealed, an interested person may declare that he had well-founded suspicions about its existence. Problems may arise, however, where those who feel it is their right to be informed suspect that certain information has been suppressed. They may also arise where there is a duty to inform others, but this has been overlooked or disregarded.

Secrecy is not necessarily a bad thing. As we have already stated, the fundamental viability of an effective counselling relationship depends upon an expectation that discussions between the child and counsellor will be kept confidential. Clearly, it is the social and legal implications of certain revelations that determine what is done with the information. Probably most counsellors would agree that there is a need to breach confidentiality in the counselling relationship where there is evidence of sexual abuse involving a child; whereas few if any would consider it legitimate, necessary, or helpful to disclose to the parents of a 15-year-old boy that he thinks he may be gay.

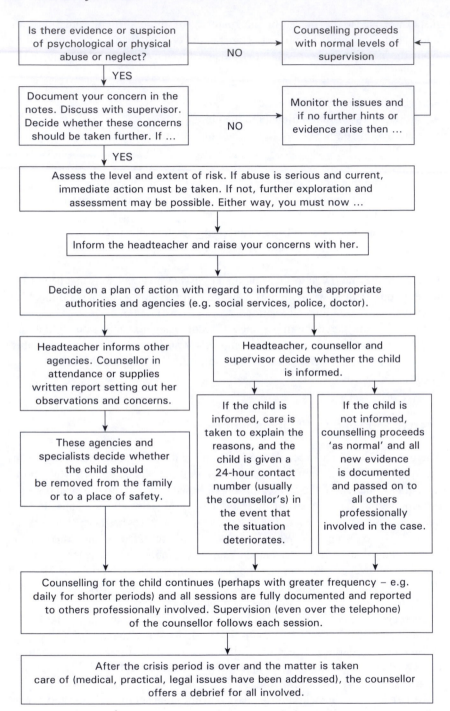

FIGURE 7.1 *Key issues in managing cases of suspected or actual abuse*

Conceptual issues

One of the most comprehensive accounts of secrets and their effects is by Karpel (1980), who examined this subject in the domain of family life. Many of these conceptual ideas are taken from his work. Secrets 'involve information that is either withheld or differentially shared between or among people' (p. 299). At least three major kinds of secrets can be described. *Individual secrets* are those in which one person keeps something private from others, be they members of the family, the health-care team, or any other constellation of relationships. *Internal secrets* are different from individual secrets, in that one other person in the constellation of relationships keeps a secret from at least one other person. Lastly, *shared secrets* are shared between those inside a constellation of relationships and information is kept from at least one other person or group outside.

Examples of secrets

- *Individual secret*: a girl of 16 keeps her worry about not having periods to her-self. She pretends that she is menstruating normally by asking her mother to provide her with sanitary towels and openly discusses issues with close friends, but does not tell anyone that she has never menstruated and feels both self-conscious and embarrassed.
- *Internal secret*: the headteacher tells the counsellor in confidence that she is being treated for depression.
- *Shared secret*: the form teacher of a 17-year-old boy referred him for counselling because he had become increasingly short-tempered following the break-up of his relationship with his girlfriend. The teacher had discussed the referral with both the counsellor and the boy.

The 'power' (or burden) attributed to the secret-holder is but one social effect of a secret. Those who are excluded from knowing can be defined as being 'one down'. Loyalty, the fear of betrayal, self-protection, altruism and guilt over disclosure are all motives for secrecy which can set up particular dynamics in the interpersonal domain. Invariably, boundaries and alliances between people are either created, strengthened or destroyed by secrets. Their effects, therefore, are at all times structural, interactive, emotional and practical.

Consequences of secrets

- *Informational*: deception, distortion, mystification, clarification.
- *Emotional*: generation of anxiety and discomfort.
- *Relational*: estrangements, violation of trust, protection, enabling people to get closer, creating new possibilities in relationship.
- *Practical*: danger of unanticipated or destructive disclosure, accidental discovery, conserve or protect relationships (adapted from Karpel, 1980: 299–301).

The effect of keeping any secret is seldom completely positive or negative, but usually a combination, although to varying degrees. A secret may bring into focus themes associated with exclusion and dishonesty. At the same time, almost all secrets serve to protect someone from something. Keeping secrets may also be a symptom of other problems. Parents of a child who choose not to disclose their son's asthma to the school may, among other issues, be denying the illness. The parents, however, may wish to protect their son from possible teasing or ridicule for 'being different'. Counselling can help people to find more constructive ways of dealing with dilemmas and facing up to the consequences of more open communication with others.

Management of secrets

Counsellors may not be excluded from the effects of secrets, which can create considerable stress and lead to a feeling of being immobilised by the client. Some may consider it their task to take sides, to advise the child or colleagues, or to expose the secret. Others may themselves generate secrets. After a child has told the counsellor that she feels she may be gay, some counsellors may prescribe secrecy by suggesting to the girl that she does not tell anyone the secret for fear of the stigmatising reactions of others. Secrecy related problems are inevitable in counselling and should be addressed by the counsellor to prevent an impasse from occurring. A number of steps can be taken in order to minimise the sometimes harmful effects of secrets. These steps are at both the conceptual and executive levels and derived from systemic theory.

Problem solving for secrecy related concerns

1   Identify whether there is a secret.
2   Identify whether there is a problem in relation to the secret, and for whom. Sometimes discussion about secrecy in general is sufficient to lead to the resolution of a secrecy related problem.
3   Clarify the dilemmas involved in maintaining the secret. Balance should be attained between the advantages and disadvantages of maintaining the secret without the counsellor necessarily favouring a position. A range of possible outcomes should be discussed with the client, using hypothetical and future-oriented questions (see Chapter 4).
4   There are several options available to the counsellor when faced with problems relating to secrets:

   - *Collusion*: agreement to preserve the secret.
   - *Challenge*: disagreement over keeping a secret with the child; the child should be advised at the start of the counselling contact that it may not be possible for the counsellor to keep secrets that have legal implications.

- *Opt out or refer:* where the secret does not have legal implications but creates an impasse in the therapy, the counsellor may suggest to the child that she would prefer to refer him elsewhere, such as to a non-school-based counselling or support agency.

Conclusion

Often, the limits of confidentiality are tested when counselling young people. It is usually desirable to inform all clients from the outset of the general limits of confidentiality. The American Psychiatric Association (1988) has provided helpful guidelines which apply to most clinical situations. These state that where another person's life is endangered by a secret, the counsellor may choose to disclose information that would protect a third party. For this reason, we do not say to children that everything they say in the context of counselling will be kept secret between the counsellor and client. The counsellor must reserve the right to discuss important information with colleagues, and the responsibility remains with the child for what he chooses to disclose in a session.

A discussion between the child and counsellor of the dilemmas incurred by secrets and their current and anticipated effects can remove a source of considerable stress from the relationship. It also returns to the child some of the responsibility for resolving problems. The use of future-oriented and hypothetical questions can help the client to consider ideas and views that they might otherwise fear to address, in a non-confronting way. This can also reduce feelings of stress in counsellor.

The presence of secrecy related problems might be viewed as an opportunity for making overt significant issues which are otherwise difficult to face. The effect of the management of secrets can itself lead to more open communication, not only between the counsellor and child but between the child and the other contacts which constitute his social group. It can also enhance the relationship between the counsellor and the professional colleagues with whom she relates.

This chapter may have inadvertently conveyed the sense that the counsellor's role and obligations when working with serious problems is confined to disclosure to other professionals. Nothing could be further from the truth. The therapeutic relationship is an ideal context in which to explore issues pertaining to loss, abuse, emotional distress, suicidal feelings and other challenging problems. For this reason, the counsellor must ensure that her legal duties do not overshadow all aspects of therapy. The following chapter describes the counsellor's role in relation to traumatic incidents that either involve or affect children.

8   Schools and Trauma

Preparation, Response and Recovery

This chapter addresses the need of a school to be prepared for and to cope with a traumatic incident. However rare and dreaded such events are, traumatic incidents are usually unpredictable and, arguably, the strength and success of a school may in part be judged by how well it prepares for, responds to and recovers from traumatic incidents. Drawing on relevant theory and several illustrative examples, this chapter describes some responses of pupils, teachers and counsellors to traumatic incidents. The longer term impact of a traumatic incident within a school is also addressed and suggestions for a disaster recovery plan are included. The presence and effective leadership of the headteacher, working in conjunction with a trusted team of staff, including a school counsellor, are crucial to the school's ability to respond to and adjust to trauma.

The School's response to traumatic incidents

Preparing for unforeseen traumatic incidents in schools is of crucial importance as unfortunately one never knows when such a tragedy might occur. The impact of a traumatic incident on a school can be devastating, with far-reaching effects and consequences. It can inevitably affect the 'psychological' health of the school and its local community. The effects on the school can persist for years to come (Hodgkinson and Stewart, 1991). However, if the school is supported through a tragedy and, in turn, support is given to pupils, staff and parents, then psychological distress may be minimised and potentially can be dealt with in a healthy and positive way. It is essential therefore to plan in advance a strategy for dealing with traumatic incidents. Planning should involve the key personnel in the school such as the headteacher, senior staff, those responsible for pastoral care, the school doctor and/or school nurse, the counsellor and parent representatives. Appropriate community-based agencies and representatives should also be included, such as social services, specialist counsellors and local religious bodies and organisations. If a crisis does occur, the disaster plan can swiftly be put into action. The benefits are clear because a staff group may not always be physically or emotionally available to give their full attention and provide specialist support when tragedy strikes.

Need for service

Horrific incidents such as the 1987 Hungerford massacre in the UK, when 16 people were shot dead by a local man, gave rise to the feeling that schools needed to be prepared in advance for the possibility of traumatic events. At the time, many schools were uncertain as to what their role was in response to traumatic incidents that affected pupils. Arguably, the emotional needs of students were neglected both in the short and long term in Hungerford (Capewell, 1999). The need for appropriate crisis intervention and counselling has been highlighted by a number of recent, severe 'high profile' disasters such as the Dunblane massacre in 1996, when a man from the local community shot dead 16 reception class children and their teacher in Scotland, before turning the gun on himself. The Omagh bomb atrocity in Northern Ireland (1998) and shootings in Columbine High School (1999) and Santana High School (2001) in the USA are further recent examples. The involvement of children in violent incidents draws immediate and prolonged media attention as the local and national community reflect on how such violence is possible. Not all incidents occur at school, though the school community may be directly affected, such as the death of 10-year-old Damilola Taylor on a street in London in 2000. These incidents distress not only the family, but also the school and wider community. The impact is even likely to extend beyond the immediate community, especially when there is extensive news coverage of the incident. Some incidents may be equally as traumatic although only appear to affect the immediate community: the tragic death of a pupil on a school trip, an accident involving a school bus, a sports injury with tragic consequences, suicide, or death due to illness are all further examples. Of course, family members, and teachers may themselves be the victims of tragic events which can seriously affect children. Sadly, ex-pupils of a school, such as those on a gap year or who recently started university may die suddenly, having reverberations through the school community they recently left. Clearly, there is a need for the issue of trauma, response and recovery, in all its forms, to be placed higher on the school agenda.

Preparation in schools

There have been some developments in the area of dealing with trauma in schools since the early 1990s. Both national and international conferences on the role of school staff after a disaster have triggered interest from schools and encouraged some to think about how they might cope with tragic events. The publication of *Wise Before the Event* (Yule and Gold, 1993) highlighted the need for crisis management work. A copy of this book was sent to every school in the UK to encourage headteachers to consider how they might respond to a tragedy. Schools were asked to develop a plan to deal with a disaster in the hope that the physical and emotional effects would be lessened.

Tragedies involving young people often evoke high levels of anxiety in all concerned. Meeting the therapeutic needs of these involved is of crucial importance to ensure that the long-term effects of trauma can be lessened. Many papers and books have been published describing how counsellors should respond to tragedies in their schools (see Grant and Schakner, 1993; Sorensen, 1989). All encourage schools to have some sort of a disaster recovery plan in place. Research developed in the 1980s has shown that children are affected by traumatic events in ways similar to those experienced by adults (Black, 1993). If children become preoccupied with a traumatic death, then the natural mourning process can be inhibited and the emotional health of the bereaved person is affected. Yet, evidence has shown that if specialist support is offered following a disaster it is appreciated and valued by survivors (Jones, 1992). Even so, one has to be especially careful when counselling adolescents. Glass (1991) points out that it is often difficult to 'connect' with teenagers because they may be masking their responses to trauma with typical adolescent reactions, such as not wanting to communicate with adults or alienating themselves from others. Appropriate interventions need to be set in place in order to allow for natural grieving and teaching staff need to be adequately trained so that they know how to respond to a disaster. Learning about children's understanding of death (Kastenbaum, 1977), the stages of grief that children might go through and their responses to bereavement (Kubler-Ross, 1983), as well as learning some basic counselling skills, would all be steps in the right direction.

Until recently, many schools had not included any kind of bereavement education for children in the curriculum. However, from September 2000, bereavement studies were added to the PSHE (personal, social and health education) syllabus in secondary schools. This has caused some controversy among mainstream educators (see Chaudhuri in *The Times*, 2 February 2000). Coping with trauma in schools has not been part of any initial teacher training programmes and teachers have complained of feeling inadequately prepared for dealing with it (Hockey et al., 2001; Leaman, 1995). Thus it is up to schools to develop their own programmes.

The Critical Incident Stress Debriefing Model (Mitchell, 1983) is useful for helping schools to deal with loss (see also O'Hara et al., 1994). This is a group intervention model suitable for systemic application in schools and based on action research following disasters. Specialists who have been trained in this method, which has a specific structure and format, come into the school to work with the traumatised group to help them talk about their feelings and express their emotions. There are three distinct phases outlined in this model: First, the group is encouraged to ventilate its feelings about the tragedy and thereby realise that their feelings are not unusual or unique. Second, the group is encouraged to talk in detail about the event, which allows the facilitators to see how intense the feelings are and enables them to provide appropriate support. Third, the group is helped to mobilise its resources and to make decisions about how to move forward (O'Hara et al., 1994).

The model can be used in planning interventions to work with parents, staff and pupils. It also ensures that the training staff are appropriately debriefed. This debriefing is necessary as it is designed to decrease distress among the mental health staff and help mobilise resources within and outside the group. This approach to crisis intervention is aimed at minimising the occurrence of unnecessary psychological suffering by allowing an individual to talk through the traumatic events in a safe and thus more structured, organised way. As a general rule, schools should take the following steps to ensure that they are prepared should a crisis occur:

1 Create a committee to set up and develop a disaster recovery plan.
2 Create a small group of teachers, parents and school counsellor to be able easily to put the plan into action if and when a crisis does occur.
3 Implement and develop in-service training for teachers and parents.
4 Implement a death education programme for the students.
5 Identify local and regional resources for support (adapted from Stevenson and Stevenson, 1996).

We can never be ultimately prepared for the unknowable, but structures can be put into place to enable us to deal with a disaster when it occurs. We would argue that the most effective crisis intervention programme is one which has been conceived and rehearsed in advance. Crisis intervention that can be planned in advance should include education on possible losses, including suicide, homicide, bomb threats and other potential crises (DeAngelis, 2000a). This should be integrated into a school counsellor's training, as well as being part of initial teacher training. Schools should consider the possibility that a tragedy may occur in their community. In order to be prepared for such an eventuality, they should prepare a *disaster recovery plan* that can be put into action should a crisis occur. Counsellors have a key role in helping to devise such a plan and co-ordinating and providing psychological support in time of need.

Traumatic stress

Most people are in some way affected by exposure to traumatic incidents, and children are no exception. The nature, range and duration of reactions is always difficult accurately to predict. These may be influenced by the nature of the traumatic incident, whether the individual was directly involved or an observer, previous experience of traumatic incidents, the presence of a relevant co-factor (e.g. an existing depression, bereavement or family dispute) and available social and emotional support. Reactions to traumatic incidents may either be (a) negligible; (b) transient; (c) prolonged; (d) delayed, though the symptoms at any stage may be similar. Acute stress disorder is a common reaction and includes having nightmares and flashbacks among other symptoms, but may last only a few weeks. Although not everyone who feels traumatised develops PTSD (post traumatic stress disorder), it is nonetheless helpful to conceptualise emotional reactions and the counsellor's role in terms of this psychiatric concept.

It is important for all counsellors to be able to recognise the symptoms of PTSD. The phenomenon had been known informally for a long time but became a much more commonly recognised and observed condition following the Vietnam war. The American Psychiatric Association gave official recognition to PTSD as a distinct diagnostic classification in 1980 (APA, 1980). PTSD was then characterised in various time stages, starting with a state of numbness while the individual attempts to assimilate the news about the stress event. At a later stage, a wide range of further symptoms may begin to manifest themselves. These may include irritability, depression, a sense of guilt for having survived and difficulties relating to others. The diagnostic criteria for PTSD are:

A. Existence of recognisable stress event which would provoke the condition in almost everyone.
B. Constant re-experiencing of the stress event.
C. Marked detachment from the everyday world.
D. Other behavioural indicators or distress including sleep disturbance, nightmares, flashbacks, guilt and avoidance of activities recalling the stress event. Overreactions to sudden noise may also occur and pre-existing emotional problems may resurface.

More recently, *DSM-IV* (APA 1984) and *ICD 10* (WHO 1992), which are based upon the earlier works but with important adjustments, have become the accepted current diagnostic criteria for PTSD although these too are in a constant state of evolution. Current diagnostic criteria are based on the work of Blake et al. (1995) and Weiss (1997) and list 17 possible PTSD symptoms of which at least six must be met and must persist for at least one month in order for the client to be diagnosed as a sufferer. Major new criteria now incorporate a sense of a foreshortened future and an inability to plan for the future, outbursts of anger, hypervigilance and a constant state of 'jumpiness'.

Until recently, it was felt that only adults exhibited symptoms of PTSD, but studies have shown this not to be the case (Black, 1993). Further research has recognised that an additional factor in the ongoing severity of PTSD is the developmental level at which the trauma occurred (van der Kolk et al., 1994). Any traumatic event at an early developmental stage in childhood may have particularly significant long-term consequences in terms of PTSD.

PTSD in children

It was noted in *DSM-III* (APA, 1980) that there were specific manifestations of PTSD in children. Although these, of course, vary from child to child, the individual may frequently display a refusal to discuss the trauma which is a separate phenomenon to an inability to remember it at all. Bad dreams may become amorphous but deeply troubling nightmares which frequently centre around recurrent themes of survival and rescue. When awake, the children may unconsciously relive their experience of the traumatic event through repetitive play. Older children may be emotionally unresponsive or have transient amnesia about the incident or forget details. Reactions may range from emotional numbness to unpredictable aggressive behaviour. A lack of interest in regular play and learning activities should be carefully monitored by school staff and parents.

The further modification of diagnosis in *DSM-IV* makes the assessment of PTSD in children even more problematic. Some children find it difficult to understand the concept of time and their notion of a foreshortened future, therefore, needs to be carefully monitored. It is useful to consider whether a child has an exaggerated concern about mortality and, in particular, whether he or she is continually questioning adults about the likelihood of death. It is, in addition, extremely difficult to establish whether a child is experiencing emotional numbing. The counsellor should be aware of developmentally appropriate manifestations of these symptoms. Children may, for instance, repeatedly act out the stress incident or manifest developmental regression in terms of thumb sucking and bed wetting, when these are uncommon in children of a similar age. Children may also exhibit a variety of apparently unrelated physical symptoms. Diagnosis in a child should, therefore, go beyond assessment of recognised PTSD symptoms and include a more global assessment of the child's emotional well-being within the areas of school, family and friends.

Children can exhibit a variety of symptoms: flashbacks of the traumatic event, sleep disturbances, panic attacks, enuresis, academic failure and personality change (Udwin, 1993). It is generally accepted, however, that children considered to be most at risk of experiencing PTSD are those who were most exposed to the traumatic event and those who have a previous psychiatric history. Symptoms can and do remain for a long time following the event. In 1991, when the roof blew off a Swindon primary school killing one pupil and injuring another, a study was carried out examining the PTSD symptoms in both parents and children following the incident and two years later (Parker et al., 1995). Many of the children experienced behavioural problems, emotional difficulties and sleeping problems (with the need to rearrange the child's usual sleeping arrangements) and some children showed an increase in disturbed behaviour two years after the event. An additionally complicating factor is that adults frequently believe a child to be unaffected by the traumatic event. In some instances this may be because the child realises that the adult had been profoundly upset by the traumatic incident and does not wish to make matters worse. As an adult, it is important to be aware of this potential silence and not to collude in it unwittingly.

Assessment of PTSD in children

In order to assess adults for PTSD, self-rating questionnaires and interviews are used extensively. Assessment of children poses additional problems (Harris-Hendriks and Newman, 1995). Age and developmental factors need to be considered. One adult needs to be nominated to provide standardised information on the child – a factor which may be particularly important if one or other parent is involved in, or has been killed in, the traumatic incident itself (Harris-Hendriks et al., 1993). An interview structured around the child, who might begin by drawing a picture or telling a story about a picture of his or her choice, can be a helpful starting point. The child's experiences of the traumatic event are then discussed at length and the interview or series of interviews is followed by closure. The child is then invited to return for another interview.

When using this method of assessment, it is important to remember that a child's concept of death will depend on age and personal factors. Speece and Brent (1984) show that young children cannot understand the permanence of death but grow in comprehension as they themselves grow older. Lansdown and Benjamin (1985) found that almost all children had a fully developed concept of death by the time they are 8 or 9 years old. Children with younger siblings have reported greater post traumatic distress (Dohrenwend et al., 1981) as do children separated from their parents during rescue (McFarlane, 1987). Udwin (1993) suggested that some studies of children failed to identify the extent of their difficulties because adults had underestimated their level of disturbance. The Impact of Event Scale (Horowitz et al., 1979) has been used with children aged 8 and over. Other tests useful for children over 8 include the Children's Manifest Anxiety Scale (Reynolds and Richmond, 1978) and the Birleson Depression Inventory (Birleson, 1981; Birleson et al., 1987) – an 18-item scale specifically developed to be used by children and adolescents. Yule and Udwin (1991) showed that this combination correctly predicted psychopathology at given months and was particularly useful for screening adolescents after a major disaster.

The Child Post Traumatic Stress Reaction Index (CPTSRI) (Pynoos et al., 1987) is an index completed by a trained adult interviewer and has been successfully used to assess children after large-scale disasters. A number of other questionnaires and semi-structured diagnostic interviews such as the K-SADS – Present Episode have also been used. This latter method requires the parents to be interviewed prior to the child and for the interviews to be videotaped and assessed by an experienced independent assessor. When screening a large number of children, methods should be simple and easy to repeat and should be implemented as soon as possible after the traumatic event. This kind of taped screening could, incidentally but importantly, also provide a documentary record which may be useful in any future legal proceedings.

Therapeutic interventions

The counsellor should not underestimate the value of talking about the incident and associated feelings with the child. Many people affected by traumatic stress report that once they have spoken repeatedly about the incident and their experiences, they improve. For this reason, keeping an open channel of communication alive and scheduling follow-up counselling sessions may significantly help the traumatised individual to recover. Over time, however, cognitive-behavioural interventions, such as desensitisation and challenging irrational thoughts, should be explored. The counsellor should either refer to or work closely with a child psychologist or psychiatrist specialising in the disorder. It is important to bear in mind that the goal of therapeutic intervention is not to help children forget what happened, but to help them integrate the traumatic event into their lives in a way that allows them to return to normal functioning as soon as possible. Those teachers and counsellors who have been involved in supporting children should not be forgotten and should also be offered support.

Disaster recovery plan

We now turn our attention to the school's preparedness for traumatic incidents and the counsellor's role in this. One school's disaster recovery plan is summarised in Box 8.1 to illustrate this.

Box 8.1

Example of a Disaster Recovery Plan

Within the first hour of a disaster

- Immediately establish one room which is the nerve centre of the school's response (usually the head or deputy head's room).
- Inform the head and management team and arrange to meet in the room.
- Inform all the staff. Some staff should be specifically prepared to take on the role of ferrying information to and from the different rooms, as and when it is safe to do so, so as to keep the lines of communication open as far as possible among the different groups of the school.
- Any pupil who has been directly affected by the crisis should be escorted to a specific room, where a senior teacher or counsellor remains. A larger group could be taken to the hall. Form and head teachers need to be with them. These pupils should be contained and reassured as far as possible as all wait for more information/directions. No attempts to seek out contact with rest of school or phone calls home are advisable at this stage until safety is re-established.
- Tea and biscuits do help to lessen physical response to shock: ask the school's catering staff to arrange food for the bereaved pupils immediately.
- Staff who are answering phone calls before the official press release should be given a brief statement that they can use for all enquiries.
- Stay in touch with the scene of the crisis, need access to mobile phones.

By the end of the first day

- A letter describing the incident and the school's immediate response must be given to all pupils to take home the same day.
- Issue press statement, ensuring it is brief and factual.
- Try to ensure that no one beyond those immediately involved has been left uninformed.
- Make arrangements with school counsellor for immediate increase in counselling support and for her to liaise with the necessary agencies.

The following day

- In the following day(s) immediately after the disaster, the head and deputy head need to be kept free to answer telephone calls. All press/media enquiries directed to the head, parents to the deputy head.
- Ensure that the pupils and staff know where and when counsellors will be available.

The first assembly

- Must be done well. Conducted by the head. The response the school adopts in subsequent weeks will derive substantially from the first assembly.

Within the first month

- Ensure that staff are offered counselling information and a meeting to help them understand their response and that of the pupils – need to understand the emotional responses that the pupils are likely to experience after trauma, give examples of how to deal with the pupils' responses.

Supporting the staff

- Make a crisis team available, including the school counsellor, local bereavement counsellors, local clergy.
- Make a crisis plan available to the staff and for administrative staff to put speedily into action. Go through it with the staff and offer training in bereavement.
- Make grief material available to staff and also to parents, including information on: grief responses, grief process, grief tasks, grief complications, grief rituals, post traumatic stress disorder, classroom discussion guide, debriefing response.
- Acknowledge feelings and provide reassurance.

Debriefing

- All staff involved in providing care and support (from catering staff, to school porters, teachers, school nurse/doctor, headteacher, etc.) should be offered an opportunity to later reflect on the tragic event(s), their feelings and thoughts about their own response to the loss.

Case study

Coping with an unexpected death

The aim of the detailed case study that follows is to describe how a particular traumatic event in a secondary school was managed. We chronicle an individual school's response to the tragic loss of a 15-year-old pupil and examine the way in which the school attempted to implement a disaster recovery plan. The difficulties that the counsellor experienced and the way in which the school responded are also described. We are extremely grateful to Sophie's parents for allowing us to write about the case that follows. (Sophie is a pseudonym.) We hope that the lessons drawn will be of benefit to others.

One of the authors works as school counsellor at a girls' secondary school. She received a telephone call at home one day informing her of the tragic death of one of the students, Sophie, aged 15, a young person on the brink of adulthood. The loss of Sophie was especially grievous because without exception everyone at school remembered her with tremendous fondness. Everyone who spoke to the counsellor about Sophie in the weeks that followed her death had personal anecdotes and stories to tell, which ranged from describing her as a tremendously caring and sensitive person to an emerging young adult who had an appetite for humour and a bit of mischievousness.

Sophie and her year group had been returning to school after an outing and she and some friends had gone on ahead of the group without permission from their teacher. On seeing the teacher and the other girls on the opposite side of the street, two of the girls turned round and ran across the road into oncoming traffic. Tragically, Sophie was killed. Her friend survived. Around 50 pupils and two teachers witnessed Sophie's body being struck by a car and subsequently awaited the arrival of doctors and paramedics at the scene. The counsellor received the telephone call later that afternoon. How then does a school react and respond to a tragedy of this kind (Box 8.2)?

Box 8.2

The counsellor's initial response

If you were to put yourself into the role of the counsellor:

- How might you respond to a tragedy of this kind?
- What sort of interventions do you feel would be most appropriate?
- What might the pupils, staff, parents, school governors be experiencing?
- What might they expect of you under the circumstances?

The counsellor's initial response

The counsellor was shocked and saddened at the terrible news and felt, in consultation with her counselling supervisor (who is independent of the school), that a team of counsellors should be brought into the school from an outside organisation such as the local child and adolescent clinic. It was already clear that more resources were needed than were available at her weekly clinic. She also did not have specialist training in post trauma counselling and was keen to solicit expert help. In addition, she felt that an outsider who was not emotionally involved in the school and its system would be more able to help her form an objective action plan. She felt that the emotional health of the whole school needed to be considered and in particular support to individual students affected by the tragedy should be offered immediately. However, the lead needed to be taken from the school.

The school's initial response

The whole school was in a state of shock. The staff followed the disaster recovery plan and set about trying to calm the pupils, ensuring that all parents were informed about the tragedy and activating the swift delivery of a brief and factual press release. The headmistress spent the day at the hospital with Sophie's parents. The school administrator telephoned the counsellor at home and told her to await instructions from the headmistress. That evening the counsellor spoke to the headmistress who gave her further details about what had happened. They thought together about what might be the best way to support the school. The counsellor suggested that a multidisciplinary team of experts be available to help effect a plan for coping with the tragedy. The headmistress felt that initially pupils should have access to staff at school, given that these were all familiar figures. She informed the counsellor that many people had telephoned the school that afternoon offering their support and specialist services, such as a bereavement counsellor, family therapists, doctors and counsellors. The headmistress was, of course, grateful for the generous offers of support at such a difficult time and agreed that they should come into school to assist with supporting the students for that first week. The headteacher asked the school counsellor to come into school especially the next day to liaise with the volunteer counsellors.

The following day

The counsellor arrived at school to meet five counsellors who had offered support to any of the pupils who needed it. Some of the counsellors were related to the pupils, two were mothers of pupils and another was a grandmother. They were shown to different temporary counselling rooms around the building and the counsellor went to her usual room. Notices were posted around the school saying that counsellors were available for anyone who wished to see one and a list of rooms and available times was also pinned up. The school counsellor was inundated with pupils by lunchtime, some in small groups, others on their own. It seemed that the other counsellors were not kept as busy. One counsellor saw two pupils, while another saw one. The school doctor did not receive any clients, nor did two other counsellors. One can only speculate that pupils may have preferred to ask for help from someone with whom they were already familiar. Nonetheless, she was grateful and reassured that fellow colleagues were in attendance. Throughout the week this pattern of referrrals continued. Different counsellors came into school and the school counsellor was kept reasonably busy. It was apparent by the end of the first week that the volunteer counsellors were no longer needed. In the meantime, the headmistress and counsellor agreed to call in some experts to help develop an action plan for the school.

The funeral and memorial service for Sophie took place on the Friday following her death. It was attended by the majority of her Year 11 group as well as many other pupils, staff members and of course family and friends. The school was closed for the afternoon. The church was overflowing with people. The choir sang and the headmistress read the lesson. The school counsellor attended the service, motivated in part by the wish to know what the girls experienced and for them to see her there. It was a very moving service.

The school was aware that such a horrific traumatic event was likely to be a major source of ongoing distress, especially for the pupils who witnessed the accident. Three children reported experiencing nightmares and flashbacks as well as other symptoms of psychological trauma and were referred on to local child and adolescent psychiatric units for assessment and special help. For those close to Sophie, such as her friends, severe grief was to be expected and the sudden nature of the loss made it crucial to provide a prompt offer of bereavement support.

The counsellor's reaction

When working in a school as a counsellor one has to be receptive to the needs of the whole school. The counsellor's role in assisting the school in the aftermath was clearly in terms of helping to co-ordinate an action plan and provide counselling support for pupils and staff. It was interesting to see that the other 'voluntary' counsellors were not fully utilised by the pupils. The knowledge that other colleagues were present and available helped to contain some of the school counsellor's own anxiety about the fact that she might herself be overwhelmed by demand. The 'over-provision' of counselling might also have been as a consequence of nobody in the school being clear as to how to react, feeling that it was difficult to refuse the many offers of help which were made. The headmistress felt that since people had willingly volunteered their services, it would have been churlish to decline and the insistence of some of the offers made it even more difficult.

At times it felt as if a level of competition displayed itself between the volunteer counsellors who had different levels of training and experience and came from different disciplines. The school counsellor felt that it was not appropriate to have family members of pupils in the school to counsel the pupils. Perhaps one could say that at the time of a tragedy people do not always think clearly or act in the most appropriate ways. With hindsight a different strategy might have been possible.

Counselling action plan

After the first week, the counsellor met with the headmistress to reflect on how pupils and staff at the school were coping. It was agreed that a meeting with a group of professionals from the local hospice and the child and adolescent psychiatric unit would be arranged in order to respond to the needs of staff, pupils and parents. The headmistress gave her the sheaf of correspondence she had received from people offering to help out. The school had begun to respond to those offering their services by saying that the school already had a counsellor in place and that she was co-ordinating an action plan focusing on the well-being of the school. The meeting of the specialists took place and various options were considered. It was concluded that the following might be appropriate:

- a meeting for the staff to help them examine their own feelings, to outline the stages or process of grief that the pupils may be experiencing and to help them respond appropriately to the pupils;
- meetings for the Year 11 pupils to give them a chance as a group to talk about their feelings and emotions about Sophie's death;
- a meeting for all parents to offer support and to allow them an opportunity to ask questions and express their concerns and feelings;
- communication with Sophie's parents to offer support and to plan with them a school memorial that may be suitable.

Staff meeting

A meeting for the staff took place in the third week after Sophie's death. This was run by the Candle Project of St Christopher's Hospice. Both the headteacher and counsellor felt that this meeting was a priority because the teaching staff had direct and frequent contact with the pupils. The aim of this session was not only to offer ideas on how to deal with the tragedy, but also to establish a forum in which staff could discuss how the school reacted and how best to support the pupils. The staff were offered an informative talk and given leaflets from Dr Dora Black's (a consultant child psychiatrist) traumatic stress clinic about traumatic bereavement, as well as information on how to identify signs of post traumatic stress disorder. They examined models of grief developed by Stroebe and Schut (1995) and looked at the ways in which people cope with grief by oscillating between confronting grief and avoiding it. There was also opportunity for the staff to talk about how they felt about the tragic loss and to ask questions. Approximately one-third of the staff attended the meeting and the feedback received about it was very helpful. The other members of staff chose not to attend and one can surmise that either they did not feel it was of interest to them and/or they were avoiding the meeting, or alternatively they may have been absent due to illness or have had after-school commitments which they could not alter.

Following the first two weeks after Sophie's death, inexplicably most girls stopped coming for bereavement counselling. The counsellor felt that this was because the girls were too upset and angry, and that their grief was raw and unprocessed. There was clearly a feeling of helplessness. Those girls who would usually come to see the counsellor to discuss personal problems may have felt that these were too trivial in the wake of such a tragedy. As the weeks went on, the counsellor continued to sit in an empty room. It felt as if she was carrying some of the anger that the school felt about this death. She felt something of the painful absence of Sophie experienced by all those in the school. Perhaps the pupils were desperate not to let slip into full awareness the immense pain they were experiencing, at least not in the form of a meeting with one employed to help students sort out painful feelings. This situation continued well into the spring term when a few sixth formers began to make appointments to see her again.

Parents' meeting

At the action plan meeting attended by the counsellor, two senior professionals from the local hospice and a consultant from the local child and adolescent unit, it was decided to offer a meeting for the Year 11 parents to discuss their feelings about the tragedy and to help them deal with their children's emotional and psychological responses. A meeting was duly arranged towards the end of term almost eight weeks after the tragedy. It was run by professionals from a local child and adolescent psychiatric clinic. The meeting was attended by about 20 parents, including the father of the child who had been killed, and was successful insofar as the parents felt that they received a great deal of support.

Communication with Sophie's parents

In the event of a tragedy of this kind, staff have to be conscious of and responsive to the parents' needs. For a period of time following Sophie's death, her parents used both students and staff to answer questions about the tragedy (sometimes at home) to assuage their grief. On occasion, professional lines may be blurred and staff must be prepared to be flexible. The parents must also be enabled to continue to have an ongoing relationship with the school, if they so desire. The school was encouraged to maintain communication with Sophie's parents, but felt it was important and necessary to refer them to a specialist agency who could provide them with the support they needed that no school could be equipped to provide. It was suggested that they contact the Child Death Helpline, which is based at Great Ormond Street Hospital in London.

A memorial at school

Two ideas for a memorial were suggested. Pupils were keen to have a physical memorial and organised a collection so that a bench could be dedicated in Sophie's memory and placed on the playground. A service took place at the beginning of the next term when the bench was dedicated and all Year 11 pupils attended. It was also suggested at the action plan meeting that a memorial service might be held in school, perhaps towards the end of the academic year. Sophie's parents also considered the possibility of an annual endowed prize in memory of their daughter.

Looking forward

A great deal can be learned from this tragic event and lessons drawn from the experience both immediately after the death and in the long term. In the first instance, it would be useful for schools to have a list of specialists, such as mental health professionals and local clergy, with their contact telephone numbers, who can be called upon at short notice if the need arises. This would be most effective if it were arranged according to area by the local education authority, but with schools encouraged to make their own contacts as well. It is important to think about the needs of three groups of people: the pupils, the staff and the parents. If nothing is done and no clear, consistent and unified response made, then the whole school is adversely affected and suffers unnecessarily. In this particular case, the counsellor felt that the needs of the parents and staff had been well met, but that the pupils' needs were not fully recognised. There was a feeling that the girls had been supportive to one another, but their attentions turned to their GCSE examinations soon after. Some girls have sought psychological support outside school on an individual basis. Where possible, details of other colleagues offering such support should be made available to staff, pupils and parents. It is entirely appropriate that pupils should seek and make use of specialist help and support outside the school.

Several years on, many girls still talk about the unexpected tragedy, but in a more resolved way. They have now accepted the tragedy and have the capacity to tell a narrative about the story which locates it in the past. Sophie's friends remember her with affection and good humour. On the anniversary of her death, flowers are tied to the lampposts near the spot where she died and special prayers recited in school. For nearly a year, the counsellor felt that she was made to represent something about the untouchability of death and the raw pain of grief. The fact that no girls attended what had been a busy counselling service led the counsellor to believe this to be the case. That time has now passed and the counselling service is as busy as ever before.

Pupils react in all kinds of ways when they experience a bereavement and this can be seen clearly from the above case example, when the death was tragic and sudden. One might have thought that when pupils are anticipating the death of somebody in their school their reaction may be different from that of a sudden and traumatic death. With this in mind we have included a further case example of how pupils in a particular school reacted and coped with the death of one of their peers, whom they knew for a while was likely to die and were thus in some ways expecting it.

Case study

Coping with an anticipated death

Coping with trauma in the case of an anticipated death can also be very distressing for pupils in a school. This case study examines the reaction of a pupil to the imminent death of his schoolfriend. Gary, a 15-year-old boy in a boys' secondary school, described what it was like when his friend Ian was diagnosed with leukaemia when they were both in Year 9. He describes how the class coped with the fear and knowledge that their peer might die and the way in which the school did respond when Ian did actually die about a year later.

> We didn't really know what was wrong with Ian for quite a while. He just kept missing a lot of school. When we found out he was so ill I think we felt quite bad. We changed our school charity to Leukaemia Research which I think was a good idea. We also wrote Ian letters and some people visited him. At one point, we thought he was getting better, but things kept changing. Then all of a sudden we found out that he had died. It must have been over a week after his death that we were actually told. I don't think the teachers knew what to do or what to say to us. There was a special assembly for the year group where we found out. People were very shocked. One of the things that was really hard was that the teachers didn't talk about death or think about what might happen because Ian had been in and out of school. I think that the teachers were very worried too, but they didn't know what to do. In the end everybody tried to ignore it and we just tried to pretend that it never happened. Nobody cried, maybe his best friends did, but definitely not in school. When he was ill some pictures of him were pinned up on the classroom noticeboard. I don't think anyone's taken them down yet. We had a memorial assembly about six months later and Ian's parents came to talk to us as well as somebody from the Leukaemia Research fund. It made people think, but then everybody just returned to normal. Thinking about it now, I think more should have been made of it. We don't have any counsellors in school, but it could have been useful if we'd had some then.

Anticipated death can be as hard to deal with as sudden and unanticipated loss. It can unnerve the other pupils and cause inattentiveness and restlessness among pupils and even result in behavioural problems. It is helpful to the pupils if teachers take a lead in helping the class decide how to deal with an anticipated death. The question of what should be done with the pupil's desk and the pupil's schoolwork needs to be considered, as well as how to ensure that the pupil's memory is preserved. When the pupil dies, his peers will still experience the usual feelings or responses to grief. They will be shocked, numb, sad, frightened or angry (or all of those things) and need to be helped to process these feelings. In the case of anticipated death, the waiting can be hard for both pupils and staff to deal with and to acknowledge.

Conclusion

There are two distinct types of bereaved children that counsellors may encounter: children bereaved in their personal lives and children who are bereaved when a tragedy strikes the school community. In each case, the child's response is likely to be influenced by their past experiences of loss and/or trauma. Counsellors should anticipate taking this past as well as the present upset into account. This chapter has considered how traumatic bereavement may affect a whole school and pointed to ways in which the school may prepare for a tragic loss. All schools need to be prepared for such events, with a disaster recovery plan at the ready, so that if a tragedy occurs the headteacher can rapidly work in conjunction with her staff and in collaboration with the school counsellor to ensure that the pupils recover quickly and the school can return before long to its normal routine.

9   Setting Up and Maintaining a School Counselling Service

The reason for having counsellors in schools is because they fulfil some essential function, which may not be provided by any other service. The school counsellor's role is to provide a safe and non-judgemental setting where children and adolescents can freely discuss personal problems and explore emotional issues that occur in their lives.

Do we need specialist counsellors?

It is important to consider who else may be able to offer support to students in school. There are a range of people in schools whose roles include pastoral care or counselling. They include: the teaching staff, educational psychologists or educational social workers, school doctor/nurse and chaplain or priest, among others. One should not underestimate the importance of informal care-giving from among peers and fellow pupils. We need to ask therefore whether a school counsellor is really necessary or if the other people around offer sufficient support and advice to the pupils.

Some correctly argue that it is the teacher who should be most concerned with counselling matters and it is true that a pupil may readily pluck up the courage to talk to his form tutor about something that is bothering him. In reality, however, there are many factors, which may impede the pupil and his tutor from achieving all of the requirements of a therapeutic counselling relationship. These include:

- time constraints;
- complexity and sensitivity of psychological issues;
- the teacher–pupil relationship may be at the root of the problem;
- the teacher's position of authority may mean students are less comfortable in a different role where greater listening skills are required;
- some teachers may feel that they are not necessarily skilled in psycho-therapeutic techniques or find it difficult to remain impartial in some situations.

When it comes to young adults, peers may be an important source of support. Peer counselling groups set up specifically for pupils who have been bullied can be especially useful (Cowie and Sharp, 1996). A mentoring system – where older pupils befriend the younger ones – and peer group mentoring have important roles to play. However, pupils often have their own issues and agendas, which may impede a broad and unbiased view of personal matters. Boundary issues also arise, for example, if the problem is very personal there may be a concern that private information might find its way to other acquaintances in the school. Again, the issue of competence and available time are potential impediments to a peer relationship developing into a counselling one.

An educational psychologist is another professional frequently called upon to consult to schools or asked to take on referrals. Many are trained to work with children who are identified as having learning difficulties or who require specialist assessment. Again, the volume of work may mean that the educational psychologist cannot respond fully to all referrals. There is also a perception that the difference between these two roles is that the psychologist is primarily focused on the 'unusual' child, whereas the counsellor is concerned with the 'normal' child (Jackson and Juniper, 1971). The school counsellor may be trained to deal with a broader range of issues and problems and have more time available for counselling.

What kind of school counsellor do you want to be?

First, it is important to consider carefully whether a school is the right setting for you. If you like working with young people and their families and with a range of problems, then a school setting may well suit you. It may be helpful to have had some experience (apart from as a pupil of course) of working in an educational setting, possibly as a teacher or school nurse. You also need to consider whether your counselling qualifications are relevant and to undertake advanced training, if this is appropriate. It is advisable to be registered with a known professional body such as the British Association for Counsellors and Psychotherapists (BACP). Accreditation with one of the professional bodies – BACP, British Psychological Society (BPS), United Kingdom Council for Psychotherapy (UKCP) – is almost a basic requirement nowadays as competition for posts is intense and well-qualified people are more likely to be appointed.

It is important to consider carefully where you would like to work. Some counsellors prefer to find a local school, as this might more easily fit with their other commitments. However, there may be some drawbacks too as you may not want to be bumping into the pupils every time you walk down the street. Think too about the type of school you would like to work in, be it a big inner city comprehensive or a local single-sex grammar school. The types of problems seen in these schools may differ significantly. Some schools already have school counsellors and additional support may be required. For others, it might be the start of a counselling service. Look out for advertisements in newspapers or contact schools directly. It may also be a good idea to contact the local education authority and find out if there are any positions available. Another strategy is to 'cold call'; for example, send letters to local schools offering your services. Describe briefly who you are, specify your qualifications and offer to meet the headteacher. It may be worth following up the letter with a telephone call. You might also liaise with the headteacher's secretary and suggest a brief meeting where you could discuss the possibility of setting up a counselling service in the school. Some schools may be interested in taking you on in their school as a trainee for a short period while they consider funding issues. One counsellor describes how she got her first school counselling position:

> In November 1998, I approached Broadgate High School by letter to ask whether they would consider taking on a trainee counsellor for a placement. The idea of a school counsellor had previously been suggested by pupils' parents and some of the pupils themselves, so the letter I sent arrived at the right time. The Headteacher, Mrs Smith, interviewed me and suggested that I should set up a pilot scheme to see whether a school counselling service could operate successfully in the school. In the initial interview Mrs Smith said that she would describe me as a Counsellor In Training to the staff, parents and pupils and that we would review the position at the end of the academic year. At the end of the year the counselling service was evaluated and deemed to be a success, and proper remuneration was arranged.

It is important to be patient when setting up something new. Most schools are responsible for their own budgets so extra funding may not be readily available. Schools may first need to be convinced that what you are offering is of benefit to the school. We are not suggesting that you should necessarily offer a free service, but sometimes piloting a service for a finite period may help you to negotiate your position more effectively. If the headteacher agrees to interview you, then we would suggest an initial consultation with her followed by a short presentation to the chair of the school's governing committee and heads of year where you could describe and promote the kind of service you could offer. This would be a time when questions could be asked and explanations given about counselling in schools. The counsellor needs to meet the unique and specific requirements of the school. In an initial meeting the counsellor could describe the following:

1 How she plans to work in the school, that is, the model of practice (without resorting to psychobabble).
2 Why she especially wants to be a *school* counsellor and what she can offer that is unique.
3 What her qualifications are.
4 The referral process and what feedback is given to staff.

The counsellor also needs to find out the following:

1 What system for psychological support is currently available to the pupils?
2 Which local support agencies are linked to the school?
3 What are the expectations of staff of a school counsellor?
4 What are the expectations of the pupils of a school counsellor?
5 How are child protection issues dealt with and who is the named child protection teacher?
6 To whom does the school counsellor report?
7 Which room is available to the counsellor and is it suitable for the purpose?
8 What hours would she be expected to work?
9 What contract is being offered?

Practical issues in setting up a service

The practical issues are very important. Getting a room that can be free from interruptions may be a challenging task in a school. Finding comfortable chairs, ensuring privacy and keeping notes in a safe and secure lock-up cupboard are not necessarily straightforward issues. If it is a part-time service and the counsellor's room is used for another purpose at other times, unintended interruptions may be inevitable. One counsellor describes how the deputy head helped her to set up her service:

> Mrs Peters turned out to be very helpful. She gave me envelopes to pin up on the door, and to put in my appointment slips. She organised the caretaker to give me two comfortable chairs and supplied me with a piece of black paper to cover the glass window so that no one could see in during sessions. She then introduced me to a wide range of people. I met the Heads of Year, the School Nurse and the named Child Protection Teacher. I felt comfortable and welcomed. It made a good impression.

Two kinds of system

Once you have established a designated working space in the school, you need to consider, in consultation with the head, what kind of counselling system you wish to operate. There are two kinds of counselling systems that can be set up in a school: the 'drop in', self-referral system and the school referral system.

'Drop in', self-referral system

This self-referral system can be usefully employed when pupils wish to 'drop in' for sessions without the school and/or parents being involved. It works by using an anonymous pre-booking scheme. In order to book a session, pupils are asked to tick a list and then to post into a secure letterbox a form on which their name and reason for coming can be written. Actual names are not entered onto the list in order to preserve confidentiality. The reasons for coming can sometimes be detailed or consist of perhaps one word, but they offer a useful guide to the counsellor. This system has proved to be successful, but can sometimes be problematic when pupils forget their appointments. However, if this happens the counsellor is then free and the door can be left open to drop-in pupils who wish to see a counsellor immediately. On occasion, the school and the parents need to be involved, for example, in the following case example.

Case Study   A 12 year-old pupil referred herself to the counsellor writing on her appointment slip the following: 'I'm going out with an older man and other stuff.' The counsellor saw the pupil and spent time talking to the child, but soon ascertained that she was having an inappropriate (not to mention illegal) sexual relationship with a man of 25. The issue was identified as a child protection problem, among other issues. She spoke to the pupil and explained that she would have to contact her parents and the named child protection teacher in school. The child was relieved that her mother would be told. She said that she was not sure how to tell her, but she was also very upset. A meeting took place shortly after this between the counsellor, pupil and parents (and the local social services were informed). Although the child was relieved that she had been able to tell her parents and that the relationship had stopped, she still felt hurt and angry about how the system had responded. A week later the counsellor received a letter from the pupil saying: 'You have betrayed me, you made me tell … I hate you.'

The counsellor's supervisor pointed out that although the pupil must have been unhappy with the situation, it was her own decision to see the counsellor. She clearly wanted another adult involved in the situation. If the pupil had not self-referred to the 'drop-in' clinic, the situation could possibly have continued for a long time and the 12 year old may not have been able to extricate herself from it.

School referral system

The school referral system works as follows: teachers identify pupils whom they feel should be referred for counselling. They discuss this list with the counsellor and the pupils they agree about (some may be better suited to see the nurse or the learning mentor) are identified. A letter is then sent home to the child's parents requesting a meeting. A meeting takes place with the following people: the pupil, his parents, the head of year and the school counsellor. After this initial consultation between the family and the school, the pupil can begin counselling sessions. A review meeting may take place after a term. This system is really most appropriate for younger children where parental involvement would be expected. Nonetheless, it can prove successful too with some older pupils. It is common to find a combination of both systems operating within a school, as this counsellor describes:

> The self-referral system works well at Thamesgate. Currently there has been a slight shift in referral patterns with teachers beginning to refer students to me. This is often done in a more ad hoc way. For example, some members of staff leave me a note in my staffroom pigeon hole (shared now with the school nurse) and suggest that I should see a particular pupil. They then arrange for the pupil to see me and book an appointment. Alternatively a teacher may suggest that a pupil contacts me direct. Sometimes teachers have helped pupils fill out the counselling form and to contact me. It is always up to the pupil to choose whether she wishes to see me. Staff also telephone me at home on occasion to discuss the best way to move forward with a particular problem or to find ways for a reluctant pupil to come forward for counselling. Of course, pupils can also self-refer at any time and parents also contact me from time to time to discuss concerns they may have.

Once the counselling system is set up and ready to start operating, it is important to ensure that other issues are addressed. Of crucial importance is the necessity to appoint a suitable supervisor whose role it is to oversee the counsellor's work in school.

Informing pupils about the service

One of the ways in which you can connect with the wider body of pupils in a school is by making sure they are informed about what is on offer in the counselling context. The counsellor can offer talks to pupils at the beginning of the school year to explain how she works. It is a good idea to talk to one year group at a time so that the pupils have an opportunity to ask questions. An example of short notes as prompts for such a talk is given in Box 9.1:

Box 9.1

Informing pupils about the service *Who am* I?

My name is _____. I am the School Counsellor. My background is _____.

A counsellor is somebody you may go to talk to, in confidence about anything that is concerning you. This could be worries about your family, anxieties about examinations, friendship issues, relationships, bullying, mood problems, anything really that you would like to talk about with a sympathetic and experienced professional. A counsellor is not a teacher in the school, but somebody who comes in from outside to work specifically with the pupils. I was asked to come into this school at the request of the pupils. Since I've been here, I have dealt with all sorts of problems ranging from issues about family relationships, sexuality and illness, to helping people come to terms with a bereavement, and many other problems on top of this. Some students just come for a single session, but others come to see me regularly for a few weeks.

How do I *make an appointment?*

At present I am here at school every Tuesday and Thursday between 8.45am and 4.00pm. I currently work in Room 4. If you want to see me, you should make an appointment. To keep the appointments completely confidential, there is a booking system comprising a tick chart and appointment slips, which are outside the room. To make the appointment, tick up on the chart to reserve your time and fill in a slip and post it in the letterbox. I am the only one who has a key to the letterbox, so you can be sure that anything you write will be kept confidential.

How can I *be sure that the service is really confidential?*

The service is confidential insofar as I do not tell anybody – teachers, family or friends – that you have been to see me. What is said within the four walls remains private. There is one main exception to this. If I am concerned that you may harm yourself or someone else or that somebody you know may be harming you, then the law requires me to discuss this with the headteacher. I would not talk to any other person without your knowledge. In other words, I would first talk to you and we would discuss which adults may need to know. My aim is to help you cope with the problem.

If you have any questions I would be delighted to answer them.

Accountability

It is important to recognise that the counsellor is accountable to the headteacher and the governors and one must ensure a professional relationship with them at all times. The school counsellor is also professionally accountable to her professional body (e.g. BPS, BACP, BAP and/or UKCP) and, as such, must strive to practise at the highest possible level in all aspects of her work, especially with regard to ethical conduct and supervisory requirements. It is the head who has a duty to care for all the pupils and is responsible for their welfare. As a counsellor, you are employed on behalf of the school to assist with the welfare and emotional well-being of the pupils. However, if something were to go wrong, it would be the head who would be ultimately responsible, even though you are held professionally accountable for all your actions (or inaction, as the case may be). It is worth mentioning at this point that it would be a foolish counsellor who practised without the necessary and adequate professional indemnity insurance.

Working in a school context is different from working, for example, in private practice. You are part of a wider system or team and directly accountable to others for your actions at all times. The school has to have confidence in the way you work. They have to know that you will react swiftly, professionally and appropriately – particularly in matters of child protection. You have to build up trust between yourself and the school. Although it will take time to do this, you can help achieve a level of trust through open communication and collaboration.

The role of the counsellor's supervisor

It is essential to find a well-qualified and experienced supervisor who has some knowledge of counselling practice in school settings. Asking colleagues for possible contacts is a first step. It may be a good idea to write to some schools to enquire whether they have an experienced school counsellor in post who may be interested in supervising you. If not, then try to find somebody who has experience of working with children and adolescents. Arrange a meeting with the supervisor and find out how she works, what her fees are and how regularly you need to meet. Keep in mind that supervision is a commitment which needs to be taken seriously and is a requirement for clinical practice and ongoing licensing/ professional registration. The role of the supervisor is to:

* monitor the counsellor's work to ensure that he is working in a professional and competent manner and help improve his skills;

- address any difficult or problematic feelings the counsellor might have in response to their client work, or feelings that have their origins in events outside school, but still affect how the counsellor works;
- offer alternative perspectives to the counsellor's work (whether with a child, family, staff or the organisation) and also validate good practice;
- help reflect on patterns of practice that might need to be reviewed or altered;
- provide a context for monitoring the counsellor's overall professional development;
- provide evidence, where required, for continuing professional registration and that the counsellor is engaged in regular supervision.

All counsellors should have a supervisor to help them manage their work in a professional manner and to reflect on difficult cases. This is particularly relevant for counsellors in school settings. Supervision is of crucial importance. A supervisor is there to ensure that work is carried out appropriately and to provide guidance and support to the counsellor. The supervisor also ensures that standards are maintained and that the counsellor's work is monitored and assessed. The supervisor should be an influential person who maintains a non-judgemental attitude towards the task and the vagaries of a school setting. It is the supervisor who emphasises alternative perspectives and viewpoints and has a sense of the pupils' needs. Supervision is also extremely useful with reference to child protection issues and knowing when to intervene appropriately.

Keeping up to date with practice issues

A supervisor should also help to keep the counsellor up to date with current issues and trends in the field. This is especially important for an in-school counsellor who may have lost links with other agencies or not be currently involved in further training. A good supervisor may also suggest further training that may enhance the counsellor's work in school. This serves to improve the counsellor's practice and maintain links within the profession. Supervision is essential for all counsellors and schools will wish to know something about your supervisor, such as how she works and how often you plan to meet. Some schools pay for supervision as part of your contract and it is certainly worth negotiating this from the outset.

It is important to get the right 'fit' between supervisor and supervisee. The supervisee needs to find an experienced and competent supervisor who understands their work setting and is properly committed to supporting them. A supervisory contract is useful so that misunderstandings do not arise.

This section has considered the reasons why you may wish to work as a school counsellor and if you are suited to the job. It has described how to approach a school and how to make a presentation outlining your suitability for the position. It has covered some of the practical issues that are required to set up a counselling service in a school. It has also outlined two different, though not mutually exclusive, ways of offering a counselling service. Finally, we have thought about how to find an appropriate supervisor and how to use this relationship effectively. We now turn our attention to qualities and qualifications required to practise as a counsellor in a school setting.

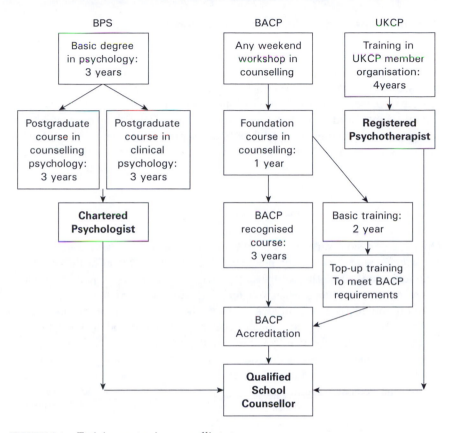

FIGURE 9.1 *Training routes in counselling*

Professional qualifications

Schools are often keen to find a counsellor who has a sound knowledge of the educational system and working with an organisation. It can be useful if the counsellor has some experience of teaching, whether in schools or universities. It is desirable, though not always necessary, for the counsellor to have had some experience of working with children. Headteachers are also interested in the kind of academic and clinical qualifications that a counsellor may have. A background in counselling, counselling psychology, psychotherapy, family therapy, social work or teaching counselling is often preferred. A police security check will also be a requirement for working with children and will be arranged by the school.

Increasing recognition has been given to the specialist nature of school counselling. A school counsellor is now expected to be registered with a professional body (such as the BAP, BPS, UKCP or BACP) and in some cases to have an advanced training, such as in the field of family therapy. Training routes for a professional qualification in counselling are shown in Figure 9.1.

Possible route options for school counsellors

If teachers show an interest in pastoral matters, they can take on further professional training. This can lead to them into a professional training as a counsellor. However, if the teacher wishes to take on a school counselling role, it is best to preserve clarity in professional tasks and not to teach in that same school. Pupils need to trust a counsellor and to believe that confidentiality is being taken very seriously. Straddling both 'worlds' is not easy, and teaching in one school and counselling in another is one way that the two roles can be kept separate and distinct (adapted from Pembroke in Bor and McCann, 1999).

The counsellor's self-development

On some occasions difficulties or setbacks may occur that make it necessary to re-evaluate your counselling practice. This could be to do with you as an individual and may influence the way in which you manage a pupil's problem. There may be situations when you feel that you cannot relate to a pupil. For example you may over-identify with a pupil: she may have an eating disorder and you may become overly close to her because your best friend also had a similar problem. Alternatively you could under-identify with a pupil and become emotionally distant. This could be due to your own fatigue and stress which make it difficult to be warm and empathic with a distressed client. Sometimes you may become judgemental about a pupil and his lifestyle. You may be disapproving because you were not allowed the same freedom when you were a teenager. Alternatively, you might recognise that you have become didactic in counselling sessions. You may be curious as to why you are treating a pupil's problem without attending to her emotional needs. One reason for this may be that as a child your emotional needs were not met and therefore you find it difficult to respond to a pupil's feelings. You may choose to discuss the reasons for your reactions with your supervisor, or alternatively you may choose to take them to a therapist. In any case you may wish to ask yourself the questions shown in Box 9.2 about your communication and interaction with your clients.

Box 9.2

Recognising unhelpful patterns in your practice

- Are you overly sensitive or emotionally cold and distant when you relate to pupils?
- Have you established a pattern which is unhelpful in how you communicate with pupils (e.g. are you frequently argumentative or dismissive)?
- Are you frequently tired and irritable (e.g. from too much work or personal difficulties)?

- Are the boundaries between your personal life and professional life unclear? Do you take home too much work, or come into work when it's not necessary to do so?
- Is there a detectable change in your leisure pursuits (e.g. too much drinking and not enough exercise)?
- Have you stopped enjoying work and do you always look forward to the end of the day?
- Have colleagues told you that you look tired and stressed?
- Have you started to neglect your own needs and interests?

If you feel that some points on the list in Box 9.2 apply to you, then you need to:

- recognise the events which make you stressed, challenged or depressed;
- recognise the patterns in your behaviour or work schedule which create or exacerbate these stresses;
- aim to reduce stress by personal and if necessary organisational change;
- re-evaluate your lifestyle and patterns of work in order to prevent a recurrence of over-stressful episodes;
- aim to improve your experience and skills so that challenges can be seen as opportunities, not threats;
- be more assertive, if appropriate;
- talk to others – discussion with a sympathetic supervisor, counsellor or peer may be beneficial.

The school counsellor–pupil relationship

The school counsellor–pupil relationship does not only exist in the counselling session, but also outside it. You need to consider how to behave when you see your clients around the school. It may be helpful to explain to the pupil in the counselling session that you will not initiate conversation or even display any gesture of recognition if you encounter them outside the counselling room, since they might be embarrassed or feel awkward. However, if a pupil comes up to greet you, then it would be rude and upsetting if you rebuffed him. Occasionally you may find that the pupil does not turn up for scheduled interviews and you need to consider why that is:

- *Forgetfulness:* sometimes, for example, at the beginning of term, pupils need to be reminded that they have an appointment.
- *Not sufficiently engaged in counselling:* this could be to do with the counsellor or the pupil, but it is worth considering if there was anything in the previous session that may have upset/antagonised the pupil.
- *Not wanting to be in counselling in the first place:* if a pupil is told that he needs to attend for counselling because he has misbehaved, he is unlikely to be receptive. Sometimes, if the counsellor acknowledges the difficulty of a pupil being 'sent' to him, the pupil might then become more receptive to the idea.

Record keeping

A school counsellor is required to keep accurate, detailed, appropriate and organised records of all counselling sessions, meetings and discussions (see Appendix B). It is important to ensure that the counsellor is aware of the school's existing record-keeping system and procedure. Most counsellors should be allowed access to a pupil's confidential records, although this needs to be cleared with the headteacher. Your own records need to be clear and easy to read and should be kept in a locked filing cabinet. Many counsellors also keep a log of all their counselling sessions containing brief details about their clients. Remember to keep this in a safe and secure place. It is important to keep accurate records of parental/family sessions. Make sure that you record the day, time and place of the meeting and who was present, as well as some brief details about the consultation session. Finally, avoid unnecessary comments or judgemental statements. Remember that, although highly unlikely, your confidential records can be subpoenaed to court and used in evidence.

The collaborative school counsellor

The school counsellor needs to liaise with a number of people as part of her job and should ensure that she maintains a professional relationship with them at all times. In this section we examine the role of the school counsellor and her position in the school and how she collaborates appropriately with the headteacher, staff and pupils. Practical hints are offered for developing collaborative working relationships with staff and pupils.

It is important that the counsellor is accepted not only by pupils, but also by staff, parents, the school governing body and collaborating agencies such as social services. It is not always possible rapidly to achieve goodwill and positive regard from colleagues and acceptance can take several years to establish. Indeed, it might be argued that, since schools are dynamic organisations and staff and pupils come and go, this acceptance is never completely attained. Counsellors therefore need to work hard at establishing and maintaining relationships with all with whom they work. This can be achieved in a number of ways:

1   The counsellor should meet regularly with the headteacher and the heads of year (she should also know how to contact the named child protection teacher).
2   She should liaise closely with the school nurse or doctor.
3   She could be involved in wider aspects of the personal, social and health education curriculum and possibly participate in personal development seminars at school.
4   She could offer to talk to parents at school evenings about general issues and problems pertaining to bringing up children.
5   She should offer in-service training to staff.
6   She could also write an annual report for the headteacher and governors, keeping them up to date with how the counselling service is developing.

The counsellor needs to liaise with a number of different people at school. It is in the counsellor's remit to take the initiative to ensure that healthy and productive relationships develop with the headteacher, teachers, school nurse, pupils, governors and parents.

When working within a school, it is important to establish a professional relationship with the headteacher. First, and perhaps obviously, one needs to be aware of personal presentation. We suggest that to maintain a professional persona, one needs to appear neat and tidy. It may be tempting to dress informally so as to appear more approachable to pupils, but there is a risk of lowering the perception of professionalism among pupils, parents and staff. Approachability and friendliness can be effectively conveyed in how we relate rather than our relaxed sense of dress. A counsellor often has to meet with the headteacher (and staff and parents) at short notice and it is important not to dress too informally. After all, counsellor is a professional role. Obviously, one must take account of the establishment in which one is working.

In terms of the hierarchy, the relationship with the headteacher should take priority over all others. Without his or her support, the counselling service may be doomed to fail or may not develop in a healthy way. It is also important to be aware of how the headteacher feels about counselling. Lay beliefs about counselling abound and some of these are inaccurate or based on only a limited or bad experience. People sometimes question the professionalism of counselling, ridicule the skills or techniques (e.g. exaggerate reflection in sessions) or downgrade the activity to nothing more than 'tea and sympathy'. Do not be surprised if there is a degree of scepticism within the school about counselling. However, the first task of the counsellor is to act professionally in all situations, including in negotiations around setting up a service. This is the most effective way to begin to counter some negative perceptions. It is useful to spend some time describing your counselling training, your skills and experience. Discuss the importance of professional boundaries and limitations from the start. Also on the agenda should be issues of child protection and confidentiality. Give examples about how you intend to work and be specific; for example, you might say to the headteacher:

> If I was working with a pupil who told me that she was being sexually abused, I would immediately speak to the named child protection officer within the school and make sure you were informed at the same time. However, if I was worried that a child was deeply unhappy about his parents' divorce and finding it difficult to communicate at home, I might work with him towards meeting with both him and his parents and having a family therapy session. In this instance, I would inform the school that Mr and Mrs X were coming for a meeting, particularly because it is on school premises, but understandably, I could not divulge the content of the session, unless the boy and the family gave me permission to do so.

Establish with the headteacher how she expects you to work and think of a few hypothetical case examples together so that the ground rules are set. It takes time to build up a relationship and gain the trust of the headteacher and, indeed, the school. One counsellor describes how she began to do this in her school:

The headmaster was at first quite anxious about having a counsellor in his school because it was new, 'something that the pupils and parents want,' he said, but clearly not something the school was committed to. However, the headteacher, Mr X, suggested, with some reservation, that I should set up a pilot scheme to see whether a school counsellor could operate successfully in the school, by offering a drop-in service to which students could refer themselves. He wrote in the newsletter to parents: 'In response to requests from pupils and parents, the school is to "pilot" a counselling scheme for the spring and summer terms only.' During the initial meeting, Mr X told me that the parents had been asking for a counsellor – 'as other schools had them' and, in effect, my appointment was made in order to pacify the pupils and parents. He liked the idea of a 'drop in' where the pupils approached me directly for an appointment, as he wanted to keep the involvement of the school itself to a minimum.

There are a number of difficulties that arise from this scenario. In terms of implementing a systems approach, it is important to work in an open system which enables the counsellor to effect change. In this particular school, there was resistance to change and a fear that the counsellor would constitute 'unwelcome change'. The headteacher was most concerned about maintaining the school's stability and the counsellor had to work hard to initiate a relationship and bring about change.

It is the headteacher's responsibility to ensure that the counsellor is introduced to the staff. His introduction sets the tone for how you are perceived by the staff as well as the pupils. One counsellor describes how a headteacher did this:

> I attended a staff meeting, where I sat beside the Head, introduced myself and explained how the counselling service would work. In this way the staff were aware of my role. I then met the Heads of Year just to say 'Hello' and make initial contact and finally I was introduced to the school nurse and the Child Protection teacher.

You might also prepare a short presentation to staff in which you expand on your method of working and practical issues concerning how you receive referrals, your working hours, confidentiality, etc. Ensure that you convey the message that you intend to work collaboratively with colleagues and that you look forward to meeting staff individually.

The school nurse and doctor also play a crucial role in the overall care of pupils and the school. It is therefore important to liaise closely with the nurse and doctor as they have an overlapping interest with the counsellor in terms of the social and psychological care of children.

> A 13-year-old girl presented with symptoms of anorexia nervosa. Her best friend was concerned about her since she was not eating her lunch in school, so she decided to talk to the school nurse. The nurse asked to see her friend, had a brief discussion with her and weighed her. The nurse suggested to the pupil that she might find it helpful to talk to the school counsellor about her worries, about her weight and self-image. The pupil agreed and the nurse helped her to set up a meeting. The counsellor saw the pupil individually for three sessions and after that time it was agreed that a further meeting needed to take place with her parents present. The school nurse was also invited to attend this meeting, since she had in fact made the referral. The meeting took place between the

school counsellor, school nurse, the pupil and her parents and a successful referral was made to a specialist and adolescent psychiatric unit focusing on eating disorders.

In this example it can be seen that effective collaboration between the nurse and the counsellor allowed for a joint appraisal of the needs of the pupil to be made and thus a successful outcome was achieved. A regular (at least termly) meeting between the nurse/doctor and the school counsellor should take place, where cases can be reviewed and concerns expressed over pupils. Collaboration of this kind helps the counsellor to feel supported and also mitigates against claims that the counsellor works in isolation. Discussion needs to take place about the importance of confidentiality, which may be construed differently by the doctor/nurse, especially in a school setting. It is therefore helpful to discuss the kinds of cases with which the counsellor has been working rather than specific details, unless absolutely necessary.

An open and collaborative relationship with other colleagues works to everyone's benefit and ultimately benefits the child. The sharing of important and relevant information reduces secrecy and rivalries between colleagues, allows informed practice to flourish, decreases the stress or burden of keeping secrets and models good practice between professionals. It is worth emphasising that non-collaborative work on the part of the counsellor can foster distrust, inflame rivalries, increase stress and may be ultimately dangerous and self-defeating in the counsellor's practice, not to mention that the counsellor will also feel alone and isolated within the school system.

Practical hints for improving collaboration in school settings

Whatever theoretical approach the counsellor uses, she will be challenged by the dynamics that exist within any school setting and by those that are unique to a particular setting. It is helpful to strive to work collaboratively in order to be valued as a team member. The 'rules' for collaborative and effective practice in school settings vary from one context to another. Opportunities to reflect on practice in a wide range of school settings through collaborative work, case discussions, peer supervision and consultation have highlighted some ways to enhance practice without straying beyond the boundaries of professional competence. Some ideas that have helped to achieve this are summarised below:

1   *Make no assumptions* about what constitutes a problem, for whom it is a problem, how people should cope with the problem, or how they should relate to one another.
2   *Practise collaboratively* as part of a team. Dispel the myth that counsellors always have their own agenda and 'get on their high horse' in order to assert their views and opinions.
3   *Be humble* but communicate directly. Learn from others and be tentative if you are unsure. Do not overstate the importance of counselling, but do not be reticent to offer directives if necessary.

4 *Learn about the school* by attending meetings, getting to know the staff and acquiring and developing an interest in the structure and hierarchy among staff.

5 *Be curious* by adopting a stance of receptive openness and asking questions. Avoid making assumptions and becoming prescriptive.

6 *Be flexible* about where you counsel the children, when you see them and approaches used in counselling for which there may be a special demand in the school setting (e.g. family therapy). Work at the child's pace and determine whether the problem is best solved by open-ended, exploratory counselling or by problem-focused counselling.

7 *Be time conscious* and aim to achieve the most within the time constraints. Learn how to do counselling briefly. When feeding back to teachers or parents either verbally or in a letter, be succinct and to the point. Avoid wordy and lengthy reports and unfocused discussions about the child.

8 *Be proactive* by not waiting for problems to occur. Waiting for the child to identify and talk about his problems and fears may extend the counselling sessions beyond their time constraints.

9 *Where appropriate, give information.* Counselling should be more of a dialogue than a monologue. Do not be afraid to give information about school rules, how the child is expected to behave and who else they should be able to talk to.

10 *Be practical.* As counsellors we are sometimes longwinded and over-cerebral in response to client problems. Learn to make rapid decisions, take small risks and think imaginatively, yet practically, about possible solutions.

11 *Respect the child's defences*, which may serve to protect them. Talk about what you observe with the child, but it is not always necessary to confront or directly challenge their defences. Counter any suggestion of blame for what has happened from either the child, school or family.

12 *Sustain realistic hope.* Therapeutic neutrality sometimes interferes with our ability to offer supportive and comforting words to the child and others. The child or family may need to hear that there will be a future after they have solved this current problem. Help them to see a future and to participate in decision making for it.

13 *Help the child to gain a sense of mastery over his situation* by involving him in decisions. Work towards increasing his choices or options. Avoid fostering too much dependence as this may be counter-productive.

14 *Evaluate your practice.* It is good practice to audit and evaluate your work. This can also help in the maintenance and development of your counselling service. Evaluation and audit of counselling practice should be initiated by counsellors, as otherwise there is a danger that others will take charge of the evaluation process (see Chapter 10).

15 *Dress according to context.* Counsellors do not have any uniform or props. The expectation of dress may differ according to school type, be it primary or secondary, state or public. Be aware of the school setting and wear something that will not mark you out as 'different'.

16 *Share your skills with others.* The accusation that some counsellors do not help others to understand more about the psychological process and counselling is not without foundation. Offer to give seminars, invite colleagues to case discussions and suggest seeing children jointly with another colleague where the child permits this. Foster a climate of openness about your work. This may help others to understand better what you do with the children and lead them to be more supportive of your service.

Conclusion

In this chapter we have examined the role and position of the school counsellor in relation to the various people with whom she works. We have considered the role of the school counsellor and her relationship with colleagues and pupils. Highly skilled counsellors may fail in their task at school if they do not heed the dynamics and hierarchies of the institution. They can also broaden their range of skills to include family therapy. Issues concerning professional boundaries, confidentiality, professional rivalries and workload demand consideration from the outset. The alert and responsive school counsellor not only recognises this and addresses these issues from the outset, but also continues to do so for as long as she works in that school. Failure to do so could inadvertently lead to institutional dynamics affecting the counselling process. Evaluation of counselling practice is an essential component of the range of engaging and collaborative activities which the counsellor undertakes. The following chapter describes how to evaluate clinical practice.

10   Evaluating Counselling
in a School Setting

We work in an era where professional accountability and credibility are expected. Counsellors working in schools, as well as those working in other settings are increasingly under pressure to produce evidence of the effectiveness of the service they provide to school governors, school principals and other school staff who are responsible for the allocation of resources, as well as to parents.

To carry out a simple audit or an elaborate evaluation of a service being provided is the hallmark of a professional approach. Feedback gathered from such evaluation provides the individual counsellor with valuable information. First, it ensures that the counsellor operates from an informed position as it provides evidence on which to base a rationale or justification for the service provided. Second, information gained through an audit or evaluation can be utilised to ensure that the service provided is customised to suit a particular school population in terms of age and ability range, developmental stages, cultural values and needs. Inadequacies in practice can hopefully be eliminated in the light of such feedback.

This chapter outlines the basic principles of carrying out an evaluation of a school-based counselling service. Although such principles have been developed in settings other than schools, they can be adapted, scaled down and applied in the often modest context of a school setting. A simple self-evaluation sheet suitable for use by children of average secondary school age is included as an example that the authors have found useful in the course of their own work (see Figure 10.1).

Many counsellors have mixed views about undertaking a systematic evaluation of their service. They may lack the confidence or skills to undertake an audit or research, or feel annoyed at having to obtain feedback from counselling service users by using methods that fail to tap into what really happens in counselling. They may have so many demands on their time that little space is left to conduct an audit. Yet, with appropriate knowledge and a positive approach, few aspects of counselling practice could be as rewarding as an evaluation that leads to an objective measure which demonstrates good and effective counselling practice.

Practitioners are now routinely asked to justify counselling in terms of cost and outcome. Questions frequently asked relate to what counselling is, what it does, who should do it, how much it costs, whether it works and for how long it should go on (Booth et al., 1997). Rather than viewing evaluation as an external task imposed on the counsellor, we hope that the ideas in this chapter will encourage counsellors proactively to set up their own evaluation projects which could then be used to justify and support their service, and the practice of counselling as a whole (Tolley and Rowlands, 1995). Before looking at how to proceed with evaluating counselling in a school setting, we first examine some of the deterrents that may be experienced when conducting service outcome and evaluation research.

Factors that may deter counsellors from evaluating their practice

There are several reasons why counsellors working in a school setting may be disinclined to initiate an evaluation of the counselling service. An emphasis in our training on the practice of counselling may make it seem irrelevant to some counsellors to evaluate what they do. It is often viewed as potentially intrusive to counselling to conduct an evaluation while simultaneously developing a thera-peutic relationship with a client (McLeod, 1994). Some counsellors may have received little or no training in audit and particularly in using quantitative research methods. Furthermore, a knowledge of single case ($n = 1$) experimental design, traditionally used in medicine or in behavioural psychology, requires extensive training (Barlow and Hersen, 1994). Where larger samples or caseloads are involved, a knowledge of how to analyse and interpret date is required. Research can also be lonely for the counsellor, especially where there is minimal collaboration with other colleagues. One cannot ignore the fact that some of the negative findings from a counselling service evaluation may be unwelcome for the counsellor. Counsellors may therefore choose to avoid research and focus instead on the therapeutic process.

Increasing demand and the need to ration services may threaten counselling services in a school. Furthermore, by avoiding a systematic study of counselling, the inadequacies of practice may be maintained. Any evaluation project can take time away from counselling activity. In busy counselling settings this may prove problematic as the counsellor struggles to maintain a balance between carrying out the evaluation and providing a cost-effective counselling service. A service evaluation which does not directly address the quality of counselling, but instead focuses on activity, may prove personally unrewarding for the counsellor.

Compelling reasons for evaluating a counselling service

Counsellors working in a school setting should evaluate their service for two reasons. First, increasingly governing bodies and headteachers demand this. As educational resources change and the demand on finite resources increases, there is a need to justify the service to those who commission and fund it. There is a danger that new or extended contracts within an educational setting for a coun-selling service will not be agreed in the absence of evidence supporting the need for that service. The systematic gathering and evaluation of data make it easier to make a case for funding.

Second, it is good counselling practice. As professionals, it is good practice to reflect on how our service grows and develops. Evaluating our counselling practice has some educational value because it appears different when we look at it systematically and more objectively. Evaluation in counselling also helps to challenge the perception that counselling is a 'soft' activity carried out by 'do-gooders' who do not have a head for figures and do not understand qualitative research methods. Counselling research can also help to challenge the mystique of what happens behind the closed door of the counselling room by clarifying the role, task and activity of counsellors. Data collected in the course of an evaluation can also provide material for publication in professional journals, particularly in new areas and specialties of counselling. Publication leads to wider exposure of the profession and may be a selling point for a service to fellow professionals, management and those who fund the service.

Evaluation can assist in the planning and development of a counselling service. It may also assist the counsellor in putting a case for additional funding to provide a higher quality counselling service. Lastly, the act of developing a small research project could improve collaboration between the counsellor and other colleagues in the school who take a role or express interest in the project.

Types of evaluation questions in a school counselling service

When evaluating a counselling service, both quantitative (aspects of the practice that can be measured in numbers or size) and qualitative (aspects that relate to quality) information are of value. A combination of the two provides the most comprehensive picture of the counselling service. It is important to note that service-related research takes place in a counselling setting and not under laboratory or experimental conditions, and therefore our methods have to be adapted accordingly. The study may be retrospective or prospective. The data can be used to give a 'slice of action' or to examine trends over time. The emphasis is on frequencies and therefore the need for complex statistics is largely eliminated. It is helpful to identify which aspects of the survey or study are best answered by qualitative and quantitative methods.

Evaluating caseload

In evaluating caseload we look at those factors which are most closely and directly related to the client.

Routine information

Routine information refers to the minimum data or information that counsellors need to collect in order to describe activity. It is advisable to agree the criteria for routine information at an early stage with the headteacher and peers, and gather the information as part of day-to-day practice. Most counselling services are required to produce some information about the range of clients who use the service. Indeed, the demand to do this within the field of education is increasing. The requirement is usually about how the service is being used and relates to indicators of workload, such as demographic details, the nature of the problems children present with and the frequency of sessions. This information is mainly quantitative. It may also include information about the time between referral and first appointment, uptake rate of first appointment, total number of sessions offered over a fixed period of 'time', average number of sessions offered to individual clients, and number of sessions not attended or cancelled. Allocation of counsellor time in terms of individual, family, staff or group sessions is an issue of interest in a school setting.

Non-routine evaluation projects

Certain aspects of a counselling practice do not require ongoing evaluation. Instead, a one-off, cross-sectional study should suffice. Non-routine projects of this kind usually arise from the following:

1   Questions about trends that are observed in a service and for which more systematic information is required to answer why the trend appears to exist at a particular time.
2   The need to ensure that a particular agreed standard of practice is maintained. For example, an audit of client notes to assess whether the agreed level of communication with school staff who refer is maintained could be undertaken.
3   A requirement to check whether changes and recommendations made on the basis of previous evaluation projects have been maintained.

Other non-routine evaluation projects may seek to explore how two or more aspects of a counselling service relate to one another. For example, a counsellor may want to establish why some children fail to attend sessions. The study could examine a number of factors relating to attendance, including some of the following:

- time waited for the first appointment
- who referred the client
- gender of the counsellor
- the range of therapeutic approaches offered.

Non-routine evaluations could also explore qualitative aspects of the service. An example would be to study the relationship between the referrer's reasons for referring a child and that child's own definition of their problem. This is highly relevant within a school as frequently more children are referred than are self-referred. This may reflect the level of understanding that the particular referrer has of the counselling service.

Evaluating the counselling service

The evaluation of the service usually refers to the effectiveness of a service and also mainly relates to administrative and practical concerns. These may include a measure of client satisfaction of administrative issues such as:

- *The actual time waited* for an initial appointment since the referral was made: Are the criteria for waiting times fulfilled? Do the clients who use the service feel they were given sufficient information about the reason for the delay in being seen?
- *The waiting area*: Are clients welcomed when arriving for an appointment? Is the waiting area comfortable? Is it sufficiently private? Is it adequately heated?
- *Location*: Were there adequate directions provided by the counselling service?
- *Counsellor characteristics*: Did the child feel comfortable with the counsellor? Was the counsellor punctual?

Many practical and administrative aspects of the counselling can be studied, but to investigate too many at the same time can be confusing and unnecessary. It is therefore prudent to list the essential factors that need to be evaluated and then rotate these so that only one or two aspects are looked at in a particular study. The following are examples of practical aspects of a service that can be evaluated.

Access to service

Most counselling services should have a fair and equitable access. A service may appear to have fair access, but experience may show that disadvantaged and minority groups are seldom represented in the same proportion to the total school population.

Effectiveness of the service as viewed by referrers

An important concern when setting up a study of referrers' views is how the counselling service can be improved or changed from their perspective without compromising the standards and ethics of general counselling. Most schools are a hub of activity and feedback about both practical and therapeutic issues is often neglected. An evaluation of the methods and frequency of communication between colleagues, the structure of counselling referral forms and the nature of confidentiality may shed light on what areas of practice might be improved.

Evaluating referral trends

Evaluating referral trends could help to clarify the extent to which different referrers' knowledge of counselling and their perceptions of what happens in sessions affect referral rates. A study may examine the range of psychological problems that a particular school staff referrer identifies and how these relate to the profile of those referred in terms of gender, race and social background. Findings could explain how gender, race and age influence the way that some school staff interpret a child's psychological symptoms. Information could also be gathered on what referrers tell the children in their care about the counselling service and process, if anything at all.

Client satisfaction

Client satisfaction surveys are probably the most difficult to conduct. The Griffiths Report (Griffiths, 1983) recommended obtaining NHS service users' opinions to monitor professional standards and this was subsequently endorsed by the White Paper *Working for Clients* (Department of Health, 1989). Some would argue that it introduces the client's subjective response to counselling, which may be difficult to measure or compare. Clients' answers are often influenced by a sense of loyalty, duty and/or appreciation of their carer. Some attempts to measure client satisfaction have therefore been of dubious validity. Although NHS client satisfaction evaluations consistently seem to demonstrate high levels of satisfaction, averaging between 75 per cent and 80 per cent, clients are prone to complain about the perceived lack of involvement in establishing goals for counselling, lack of choice of treatments received and the time delay between the referral and initial appointment (Brant, 1992). It is essential to include items in a school evaluation about those aspects of the service that children feel could be improved. Valuable opportunities may be lost if children feel that their opinions and experiences are not sought and acted upon.

Although all these issues are important to consider when preparing a client satisfaction study in a school counselling service, the questionnaire in Box 10.1 illustrates a very basic evaluation instrument that can be used. The sections of the questionnaire are as follows:

A *Referral process*: the answers to these questions provide information about the referral procedures.
B *Practical issues*: This section provides information about the counselling environment. Questions should be limited to those aspects which can be changed or improved.
C *Process of treatment*: this provides information about the subjective experience of the counselling process.

Remember to keep the questionnaire reasonably short and comprehensible to the youngest of the service users. It is offputting to the child to have to complete a long survey. Also ensure that it is checked for spelling, accuracy and readability before giving it to children to complete.

Box 10.1

EVALUATION FORM

A   Referral process

1   How did you find out about counselling at school?

Welcome talk   ☐   Tutor   ☐   Friend   ☐   Other   ☐   Please state:

----

2   How long did you have to wait for an appointment?

Same day   ☐   Same week   ☐   More than a week   ☐   More than
two weeks   ☐

B   Practical issues

1   How satisfied were you with the waiting area?

Very satisfied   ☐   Satisfied   ☐   Dissatisfied   ☐   Very dissatisfied   ☐

2   Did you feel satisfied with the reception when you arrived for your
appointment?

Very satisfied   ☐   Satisfied   ☐   Dissatisfied   ☐   Very dissatisfied   ☐

3   How satisfied were you with the counselling/advice?

Very satisfied   ☐   Satisfied   ☐   Dissatisfied   ☐   Very dissatisfied   ☐

4   Were you offered an appointment at a convenient time?

Very convenient   ☐   Convenient   ☐   Inconvenient   ☐   Very
inconvenient   ☐

C   Process of treatment

1   Did you feel UNDERSTOOD by the counsellor?

Very understood   ☐   Understood   ☐   Not understood   ☐
Misunderstood   ☐

2   Did you feel RESPECTED by the counsellor?

Very respected   ☐   Respected   ☐   Disrespected   ☐   Very disrespected   ☐

3   Do you feel that the counselling was useful?

Very useful   ☐   Useful   ☐   Not useful   ☐   Unhelpful   ☐

4 Is there anything you would like to be different?

Thank you for taking the time to share your views.

Assessing the value of counselling

An area of evaluation that counsellors sometimes avoid is that of assessing the effectiveness of their therapeutic work. The questions that counsellors need to be asked are about outcome: *Who* should judge the outcome, *when* in the therapeutic process should it take place and *what* questions may help in preparing this type of evaluation:

- Should the counsellor, teacher, parent or child judge the outcome and standard of counselling?
- Should the evaluation take place during the counselling process, at the time of the last session, or later?
- Should the goals that are set in the counselling sessions be used to assess the standard of counselling and, if so, do the counsellor and child need to agree on the goal?

It is desirable to link outcome of counselling to factors such as the presenting problem and the length of counselling involvement (Hewson, 1994). It is also helpful to go back to the main evaluation question from time to time when deciding which of these factors should be included and which excluded in a particular project. The outcome of counselling needs to be studied in relation to a broad range of measures in order fully to assess the impact. Noting what other researchers have done in NHS settings and incorporating their ideas into your study can help to save valuable time (Table10.1).

A method of measuring outcome is through the Goal Attainment Scale (GAS), used by Kiresuk and Choate (1994) and more recently by Booth et al. (1997). In contrast to standardised scales which assess clients on the same dimensions, the GAS allows change in individual clients to be measured in relation to specific symptoms orproblems that are targeted in the intervention. The application of this in school counselling clearly illustrates the value of this approach. Goal setting is an individual measure, a way of making the expectations of individual clients more explicit, which then allows for qualitative comparisons as opposed to quantitative measures between individuals on the same scale. It further allows for the individual perspective and requirements of the child to be incorporated into the study. Simply but concisely: before counselling, the child is asked 'What do you want?' and after the counselling, 'Did you get it?' (Booth et al., 1997).

TABLE 10.1   *Examples of studies and papers on client satisfaction and outcome*

Publication	Themes of evaluation and outcome
Booth, H. et al. (1997) 'Process and outcome of counselling in general practice', *Clinical Psychology forum*, 101: 32–40.	Questionnaires evaluating: GP consultations, referrals to other mental health services, quality of life, problem resolution, goal attainment, goal setting.
Clarke et al. (1994) 'The development of an outcome audit programme for five therapy professions: evaluating the evaluators', *Clinical Psychology Forum*, 70: 26–31.	Interviews: facilitating the therapist-led audit; evaluating outcome audit programme; future of audit projects.
Halstead, J. (1996) 'Psychotherapy outcome audit: what is not going on?', *Clinical Psychology Forum*, 90: 5–7.	Fear of not detecting change; post-therapy measures; equation of outcome audit with power; fear that outcome will show psychotherapy to be ineffective; problems of dissemination.
Neilson, J. (1994) 'Therapist–patient concordance on therapy process and outcome and its implications for service evaluation', *Clinical Psychology Forum*, 73: 5–7.	Therapist/patient evaluations: helpful versus unhelpful aspects of therapy; patient satisfaction; different perspectives, values and degrees of importance attached to events occurring in therapy.

Steps in setting up an evaluation of counselling in a school setting

It is important to take charge of the evaluation process at an early stage to avoid the danger of other stakeholders imposing their own questions and emphasis on the research. This could reflect what is meaningful for them rather than address what is appropriate for the counsellor. The following sequence of steps could be followed in setting up and undertaking research.

- *Step 1*:   Establish what *information* is needed to increase your knowledge of the counselling practice that would confirm certain aspects of the practice or that may lead to changes.
- *Step 2*:   Establish what *questions* need to be answered. Decide whether these questions could be broken up into smaller or less complicated questions. Take care not to ask too many questions; further aspects could be studied at a later stage.
- *Step 3*:   Explore *further ideas* by reading through published literature for similar and related studies. This may also be instructive in relation to methods used. Valuable time can be saved by using or modifying existing measure. Remember always to acknowledge the original author of a questionnaire. Many registered and standardised published questionnaires can only be used if the counsellor is registered with the relevant test publishing company.

- *Step 4*:   *Methods*. Decide which existing measures could be used to answer the evaluation questions. This will also be influenced by the age group of clients seen and their level of comprehension. Questionnaires such as the Beck Anxiety Inventory (BAI), Beck Depression Inventory (BDI), Beck Hopelessness Scale (BHS) and the General Health Questionnaire (GHQ) are some standardised questionnaires that are used, either on their own or in combination with your own locally developed questionnaire adapted for use with school-age children (see Table 10.2). If the standardised question-naires do not answer all the questions, you may wish to develop your own questionnaire which is specific to the questions and your particular practice. Ideally, questionnaires should be standardised. Ask an experienced researcher to help you with this. Make sure that a small sample of clients is used to pilot your questionnaire so that obvious mistakes and ambiguities can be eliminated.

- *Step 5*:   Write up a *preliminary proposal* to help provide a structure and proce-dure for carrying out the study. This also provides evidence that the counsellor will endeavour to approach the task systematically and has anticipated stages and problems involved in the process of evaluation.

- *Step 6*:   Negotiate and encourage *participation* with colleagues in the school, prior to and during the planning of the study. The discus-sions should include the use of school and counselling facilities, equipment, availability and use of a database or files and time allo-cation for the study. It is essential first to consult with the head-teacher to gain access to non-routine school facilities and school records, and to involve colleagues at an early stage of the evaluation process so that their ideas can be taken into account. This may also reduce resistance to a project. It is important to ask other colleagues in the school whether they want to include any questions. Remember to deal with issues of authorship from the outset if a paper is likely to be produced. Failure to do so can contaminate relationships with professional colleagues and lead to an unwilling-ness or resistance to participate in future projects.

- *Step 7*:   Now write up the *final proposal*, taking into account what you have gained in the previous steps. The following headings could be used in writing up the evaluation proposal:

  - Background to the proposal
  - The research questions
  - Sampling
  - Methods: what measuring tools will be used to gather information?
  - Analysis of information: this section should include how the information will be analysed, by whom and which statistical methods will be used
  - Feedback methods: this may include plans for publication.

TABLE 10.2   *Examples of existing instruments for use in NHS primary health care evaluations*

Measure	What it does?
Beck Anxiety Inventory (BAI)	Measures the severity of anxiety. It evaluates both the physiological and cognitive symptoms of anxiety. 21 items, takes 5–10 minutes to complete.
Beck Depression Inventory (BDI)	Designed to assess the severity of depression. Also used as a screening instrument for detecting depressive symptoms. 21 items, takes 5–10 minutes to complete.
Beck Hopelessness Scale (BHS)	Measures the extent of negative attitudes about the future (pessimism), loss of motivation and expectation. 20 items, takes 10 minutes to complete.
Therapy Evaluation Questionnaire (TEQ), developed from the Evaluation Questionnaire (Stiles, 1980)	Assesses whether therapy is valuable/worthless on a 7-point scale.
Helpful Aspects of Therapy Questionnaire (Neilson, 1994)	17 items, helpful or unhelpful aspects of therapy.
General Health Questionnaire (GHQ)	Designed to be a self-administered screening test aimed at detecting psychiatric disorders, particularly psychological components of ill health.
Cross-Cultural Inventory Scale Revised (CCI-R)	Assesses counsellor's ability to work effectively with diverse racial/ethnic groups. Three areas are assessed: cultural awareness and beliefs; cultural knowledge; cross-cultural skills.
Goal Attainment Scale (GAS) (Booth et al., 1997)	Assists patients in establishing one to three goals and rating each goal.

Note: Most of these tests are suited to older adolescents and adults rather than young children. Although most tests can be administered under supervision, they should only be interpreted by professionals with appropriate clinical training and experience according to the guidelines of the registering and issuing bodies.

- *Step 8:* *Sampling.* It is important to decide what criteria will be used to select participants in the evaluation. This is usually based on what will best answer the questions that are of interest to the counsellor. You will need to decide whether all children using the service over a particular time period will be approached or whether the questionnaire will be given to a sample of those who use the service.
- *Step 9:* *Gathering data.* Once everyone has been consulted and the study has the support of all the relevant people, data collection can begin. Different methods of data gathering may be used, each ideally chosen to suit the specific project. For example, structured interviews,

semi-structured interviews or questionnaires are typically used. Each has its advantages and disadvantages (see Barker et al., 1994). Data can, of course, also be collected from a number of different sources. Some of this can be done without the direct involvement of children and may entail looking at school records or counselling service files or consulting a client database. Structured questionnaires can also be sent to previous service attendees, although this may raise questions about protocol and ethics if those who have been discharged are contacted without being forewarned at the time of attending the counselling service.

- *Step 10*: *Analysis of the data*. Consider the cost of data collection, both in relation to time and resources. It may be more cost effective for administrative staff to add up lists of numbers (frequencies) manually, while the counsellor concentrates more on data and the analysis.

- *Step 11*: *Feedback to clients and colleagues*. An important part of a study is concise and clear feedback to service users and colleagues. Client feedback could be in the form of a poster in the waiting area or, for example, the school magazine or a copy of a shortened version of the full report. For school governors, both a written report and short presentation may be of value. Oral presentations facilitate discussion about the meaning and outcomes of the evaluation and consequent action plans.

Conclusion

Service-related research is a means of reflecting on the whole therapeutic process while at the same time satisfying the needs of school governors, the headteacher, children and referrers. It also opens up possibilities for collaborative research with colleagues. Counsellors working in schools are under increasing pressure to respond to demands for evidence-based practice. Most counsellors share the view that the efficacy of counselling cannot be evaluated in a reductionistic way, similar to the double-blind, placebo-controlled trials carried out in medicine. To dismiss studies of counselling activity and process, however, is both naive and self-defeating. Indeed, the development of counselling in schools depends on research. Numerous studies of counselling in different contexts are now under way in the UK, the results of which will help us to understand what happens in counselling and what makes it effective. Outcome research conducted across a range of settings, as well as more modest counsellor-led, in-house audit initiatives, all add to our understanding of these issues. This chapter serves to introduce counsellors to service-related research and the pleasures (and challenges) associated with this.

Appendix A

Confidentiality: Counselling and the Law

Confidentiality is one of the most fundamental ethical obligations owed by counsellors to their clients. The Code of Ethics requires that 'Counsellors offer the highest possible levels of confidentiality in order to respect the client's privacy and create the trust necessary for counselling' (BAC, 1997: A3). This ethical obligation and the more detailed guidelines for practice (BAC, 1997: B3) follow the current legal requirements as they apply to counsellors. Both the ethical and legal requirements have developed out of the recognition of a wider social and moral obligation to protect personally sensitive information which has been disclosed confidentially or in private. The moral and legal assumption is that professionals like doctors, priests, counsellors and others require a considerable degree of personal frankness on the part of those who seek their services in order for the help to be effective and that this creates a corresponding obligation to protect those confidences from unauthorised disclosure. This general principle is probably both widely understood and supported. However, the application of this principle quickly reveals a considerable degree of complexity as other considerations are taken into account. This complexity is reflected in the current state of the law.

Counsellors who seek to inform themselves in more detail about the current law on confidentiality will encounter a number of difficulties. First, the law of confidentiality is evolving rapidly. Initially, the courts protected information about the family, especially sexual behaviour within marriage[1], and financially sensitive information about commercial or manufacturing processes[2]. However, the doctrine of confidentiality is not limited to those fields and has been substantially widened. The current law of confidentiality covers any relationship within which there is a recognised public interest in fostering free exchange of information between parties and avoiding the fear of disclosure to others which might inhibit frankness (Feldman, 1993: 435). The second difficulty is the absence of any single coherent approach to confidentiality, especially in Britain where the courts have taken a pragmatic and flexible approach in response to problems as they have arisen (Curry, 1985: 59). The recommendations of a Law Commission on Breach of Confidence (1981) which might have brought a more systematic approach to the law were not enacted as legislation. Instead, the law seems likely to continue to develop within different and only partially compatible approaches. Internationally, different approaches to confidentiality have tended to be constructed around a primary concept of legal privilege, a right to privacy or protection of personal information. All three approaches co-exist within British law.

The most important legal approach to confidentiality for counsellors in Britain is the protection of personal information. 'Personal information' has been defined as consisting of 'those facts, communications or opinions which relate to the individual which it would be reasonable to expect him or her to regard as intimate or sensitive and therefore to want to withhold or at least to resist their collection, use or circulation' (Wacks, 1989: 26). This approach stands in contrast to a European approach which emphasises a right to privacy and may become more influential in Britain if proposals to adopt the European Convention on Human Rights and Fundamental Freedoms (1950) are enacted by Parliament. S.8 of the Convention protects the right to respect a person's private and family life, home and correspondence. The concept of legal privilege is of limited interest to counsellors as providing protection of confidences when the counsellor seeks legal advice but is of little direct relevance to the relationship between counsellor and client (except possibly in marital counselling concerning separation or divorce – see Jenkins, 1997: 168). In Britain, legal privilege has been largely restricted to protecting confidences between clients and their solicitors or barristers from disclosure during legal proceedings. This contrasts with the law concerning therapists and doctors in many states in USA which gives them the legal privilege of *not* giving evidence in a court concerning a client or patient (Bollas and Sundelson, 1995: 11). The coexistence of different approaches to confidentiality undoubtedly makes for a complicated and fragmented legal approach to confidentiality in which it is sometimes difficult to be certain about how the law would be applied in a case involving a counsellor. In this respect, counsellors are in no worse position than any other new profession and may be in a better position than many. In the absence of clear case law, the British Association for Counselling has sought legal opinion, through Kenneth Cohen solicitor, from John Friel, a barrister, on two occasions. These legal opinions have been taken into account in the preparation of this information sheet.

The legal basis for confidentiality about counselling

A legal obligation for counsellors to protect the personal confidences of their clients has been founded on several different sources of law and on different lines of argument including:

(a) Common law and equity

It is not unusual to find that there is little doubt about the existence of a legal obligation of confidence being owed in common law and/or equity without the support of extensive legal authority on the point[3]. Courts have tended to move directly to consideration of allegations of breach of confidence, without finding it necessary to establish the existence of a duty of confidentiality in general terms (Kennedy and Grubb, 1994: 638). In the absence of a duty of confidentiality arising in contract or by statute (see later) the courts have recognised that a duty of confidence exists when:

(a)   information is disclosed by someone who explicitly states that the communication should be treated confidentially, or
(b)   someone accepts a communication in confidence, and
(c)   it would be just in all the circumstances to prevent disclosure of that information[4].

In the first incident presented for legal opinion by BAC, student counsellors were facing demands that Her Majesty's Inspectors be allowed to directly observe counselling sessions with students. Legal opinion (Friel, 1992) confirmed that this was an unjustified demand which could only be justified by express statutory powers in order to override the common law obligation of confidentiality. The HMIs did not possess such powers.

The second set of circumstances presented for legal opinion raised another aspect of the common law concerning the nature of the relationship between counsellor and client. Colleges of further education were instructing student counsellors to report all suspected or disclosed incidents of child abuse. The college authorities based their instruction on the public interest in preventing or detecting child sexual abuse, which they considered override any obligation of confidentiality. Legal opinion from John Friel disagreed with this view. His opinion was founded on the nature of the relationship between counsellor and client where one person is in a position of trust relative to another, a relationship known as 'fiduciary' in legal terminology. Drawing upon one of the fullest statements about medical confidentiality[5], which would be equally applicable to counselling, attention was drawn to the judge's explanation for the confidential nature of the relationship:

> *'Without trust [the doctor/patient relationship] would not function properly so as to allow freedom of a patient to disclose all manner of confidences and secrets in the practical certainty that they would repose with the doctor. There rests with the doctor a strong ethical obligation to observe very strict confidentiality and hold inviolate confidences and secrets he receives in the course of his professional ministerings. If he adheres to that principle then the full scope of his ability to administer medical assistance to his patient will develop.'*
>
> *Jeffries J. also recognises that there may be circumstances where a doctor is required by law to disclose such information where a doctor may exercise his professional judgement in circumstances where another's life is in danger of harm, if he really believes such a danger exists. In such circumstances the doctor must act unhesitatingly to prevent injury even if there is to be a breach of confidentiality. Jeffries J. then stated:*
>
> *'However, the qualification cannot be advanced so as to attenuate, or undermine, the immeasurably valuable concept of medical confidence. If it were applied in that way then it would be misapplied, in my view, because it would be extravagant with what is essentially a qualification to the principle. Some might say that is an exercise in line drawing and if they do, so be it. The line drawing is not arbitrary but based upon reason and experience, and it is the exercise of professional judgement which is part of daily practice for a doctor.'*
>
> *I take the view, that on the basis of the concerns of my clients, the colleges are not in a position to impose disclosure as they appear to be doing in practice. In so doing they are going over the 'line' drawn by the law in this situation.* (Friel, 1998: 4–5)

It follows that in protecting the fiduciary relationship from unwarranted demands for breach of confidence the legal responsibility for decisions about confidentiality rests with the counsellor personally who must use professional judgement according to all the circumstances of the case. The counsellor must also be prepared to be personally accountable for the decisions made, if they are challenged by a complaint to a professional organisation or in the courts. The detailed provisions within the code for counsellors (BAC, 1997) require a standard of practice consistent with honouring the level of trust required in a fiduciary relationship. Any limitations of confidentiality should be kept to the minimum (B3.1), and specifically authorised by the client's permission (B.1.3.7) or clearly communicated as a prior condition of offering counselling (B.3.3.1) to which the client has agreed. Legal and ethical provisions where the balance of interest permits or favours disclosure are considered below.

One major recent development in common law has been the increasing recognition of the rights of children and young people of 'sufficient intelligence and understanding'[6] to receive confidential counselling. The law relating to young people (i.e. under the age of 18) has always sought to balance the self-determination and protection of young people. This remains the case following the landmark case of Gillick (1985) which decisively moved the balance in favour of a young person's right to self-determination. Since Gillick, there have been a series of judgements limiting those rights and sometimes seemingly contradicting both legislation and case law (Bainham, 1993: 276–90) where the court considered protection was in the best interests of a particular young person[7]. The willingness of courts to be pragmatic and flexible concerning confidentiality and adults, is even more evident with young people. This creates a degree of uncertainty for counsellors about the current law which is still evolving. A counsellor who can demonstrate having made a conscientious decision in the best interests of the young person concerned is much better placed legally than someone who adopts an inflexible stance favouring either self-determination or protection. Some legal principles can be used to inform the decision. There is a strong ethical argument for ensuring that young people survive to adulthood when they are considered responsible for deciding their own destiny. As a consequence the courts are unwilling to allow a young person under the age of 18 to refuse life saving treatment. However, this reluctance to permit a refusal to life saving treatment falls short of creating either a general duty to rescue or the right to override a young person's refusal of treatment without a court order or other statutory authority. In each case the authorities went to the courts in order to seek authority to impose treatment against the wishes of the young person concerned, thus indicating the importance attached to a young person's consent or refusal. In most other circumstances, 16–18 year olds are considered legally competent under S.8(1) Family Law Reform Act 1969 to consent to or refuse medical treatment or confidential counselling without reference to a parent[8]. For under 16 year olds, the Gillick test of 'sufficient understanding and intelligence' to receive confidential counselling applies. There is disagreement about what this means in practice. Lord Scarman gave little guidance on how to determine 'sufficient intelligence and understanding' and his judgement has been interpreted to mean that the parental rights end when the child is assessed as competent. (Bainham, 1993: 279; Children's Legal Centre, 1997: 2). A different view was taken by Lord Fraser in the same case who considered that the ending of parental rights was less clear cut. He suggested that parental involvement in decisions involving competence in young people to proceed with counselling without parental notification or consent should be assessed according to five criteria. I have adapted these so that they apply more directly to counselling. The young person

(1) should be capable of understanding the counselling,
(2) cannot be persuaded to inform parents or allow the counsellor to do so,
(3) is likely to begin or continue behaviour with serious consequences (e.g. sexual intercourse),
(4) is likely to experience deterioration in physical or mental health unless counselling is offered, and
(5) the best interests of the young person require the provision of counselling without parental consent.

The last criterion is probably the most important and therefore the one around which the relevance of the other criteria should be considered. If a person under 16 is not considered 'Gillick competent' parental consent to counselling should be sought. The consent of one parent is sufficient. It is permissible to provide counselling in an emergency situation without parental consent, but a parent should normally be informed afterwards. An obvious exception to involving a parent would be where the counselling concerns allegations of abuse by a parent, in which case careful consideration of the 'best interests' of the young person is required. Although there is no general legal duty to disclose allegations of abuse to the authorities, it may be appropriate to consult the NSPCC, Social Services, the Police or to seek legal advice from a solicitor or the Children's Legal Centre. Conscientious use of counselling supervision and seeking appropriate legal advice are important aspects of good practice in this challenging area of counselling.

(b) Contract

Contract is a distinctive area of law. It is of particular relevance to counsellors working with clients who pay a fee (however nominal) for their counselling or who provide a service in return for counselling. A legally enforceable contract requires 'consideration' (e.g. payment or the promise of payment or services) and agreement. The reaching of an agreement about confidentiality between counsellor and client is the best protection for both parties. From a practical point of view, it is much easier for a client to enforce a contractual term of confidentiality because the matter can be heard at a local County Court with relatively user-friendly procedures and low costs in comparison to seeking to enforce confidentiality arising from other areas of law (Law Commission, 1981: 83–4).

Pre-counselling information sheets, written contracts and contemporaneously recorded details of agreements in case notes are all useful sources of evidence about the agreement concerning confidentiality. Personal recollection given as oral evidence is more vulnerable to contradiction and uncertainty. The presumption that counselling is a confidential relationship is sufficiently strong that the courts will imply a term of confidentiality within a contract where this has not been explicitly and clearly agreed. As the exact nature of a term which is implied by a court must be less predictable than one reached by agreement, it is in both the client's and counsellor's interests to have reached a clear agreement.

It is ethically and legally unwise to promise 'total' or 'absolute' confidentiality. 'Confidential counselling' or the simple statement 'counselling is confidential' is more appropriate to circumstances in which the counsellor wishes to offer the highest level of confidentiality. An alternative would be to offer 'the highest level of confidentiality consistent with the law and the codes of the British Association for Counselling' (or other appropriate professional body). This would protect a client from the voluntary disclosure of confidences without the client's permission, unless legally or professionally required to do so. For example, a court order but not a solicitor's letter requesting information would be required to justify a disclosure. Professional requirements are defined by the relevant code which ought to be available for clients to consult. Any further limitations can be included as contractual terms. (For a more lengthy consideration of possible forms of words in client information sheets and agency policy see SCODA, 1994: 14.)

Counsellors working in agencies need to consider the compatibility between two contracts, namely any legal contract with their client and the contract with the agency, usually a contract of employment. Although there is no clear legal authority, it is well established that compliance with a requirement of a contract of employment is no defence to an action for breach of confidence. The Law Commission (1981: 52) considered the following example:

> *a doctor or a psychologist employed in industry is faced with a demand by his employer for the disclosure of medical records relating to other employees of the firm who have frankly discussed their personal problems with him on a confidential basis and without any express or implied understanding that the information would be made available to the employer.*

The Law Commission decided that provided no question of public interest (e.g. health and safety of other employees) was at stake, the doctor or psychologist [or counsellor] must preserve the confidences. Only an express or implied limitation on the degree of confidentiality between the counsellor and client compatible with the contract of employment would permit the necessary disclosure.

With regard to a requirement on counsellors to report all instances of suspected child abuse, John Friel stated,

> *A contract which obliges disclosure in all cases where abuse is suspected or reported has in my view the effect of abrogating the duty of confidence. It effectively places the duty on the counsellor to disclose in all circumstances where some sort of abuse is reported, outside the law of confidentiality, without any consideration of their own professional judgement and duty... It would also be a breach of their fiduciary duty.* (1998: 7)

He concluded,

> *While I always take the view it is always unwise to try and define all circumstances in which such a duty to disclose will arise in a confidential situation, it is clear that the normal situation is where the counsellor discovers a risk to the public, or a risk to the student. In all the circumstances that must involve an element of professional judgement.* **Contractual arrangements which go beyond this, are clearly vulnerable**

to challenge both in judicial review and indeed private law claims. This is not least by the students themselves. On a practical basis it must be appreciated that most students will be eligible for legal aid. They have very valid reasons for protecting their own confidentiality in relation to issues of this nature. (Friel, 1998: 8 – emphasis added)

(c) Statutory protection of confidences

The Police and Criminal Evidence Act 1984 provides explicit and wide-ranging protection for counselling records during police investigations. The Act creates three levels of protection named as privileged, excluded and special. The middle category is explicitly relevant to counselling as protecting 'personal records' which are defined in S.12 as:
documentary and other records concerning an individual (whether living or dead) who can be identified from them, and relating –

(a) *to his physical or mental health;*
(b) *to spiritual counselling or assistance given or to be given to him;*
(c) *to counselling or assistance given to him, for the purposes of his personal welfare, by any voluntary organisation or by any individual who –*

> (i) *by means of his office or occupation has responsibilities for his personal welfare;*
> *or*
> (ii) *by reason of an order of court, has responsibilities for his supervision.*

These records are 'excluded' from the powers of the magistrate to issue search warrants which instead must be issued by a circuit judge. The aim is to protect the reputation of the professional or voluntary counsellor for preserving confidences and other innocent clients against invasion of privacy by the Police, rather than to protect the confidences of the client under investigation (Feldman, 1993: 454).

The Human Fertilisation and Embryology Act 1990 created statutory authority for a Code of Practice which offers special protection for counselling records in that setting. Paragraph 6.35 requires that 'All information obtained in the course of counselling should be kept confidential' (HFEA, 1993: 33) except

> *If a member of the team receives information which is of such gravity that confidentiality cannot be maintained, he should use his or her own discretion, based on good professional practice, in deciding in what circumstances it should be discussed with the rest of the team.* (HFEA, 1993: 16 para. 3.27)

Remedies and penalties for breach of confidence

Courts have a variety of remedies for breach of confidence. The injured party can sue in order to obtain a court order, known as an injunction, to prevent breaches of confidence. The court may also award damages, especially if the client is fee-paying. The damages may be substantial if it can be shown that there was damage to social reputation, severe injury to feelings, job loss, reduced prospects of promotion etc. Damages may be awarded even if the client has not suffered financial loss because there may be no better way of acknowledging the harm that had been done. A judge has speculated that imprisonment would be an appropriate penalty for a health worker who leaked the names of doctors with AIDS to the press[9].

These remedies or penalties will not apply if either the breach of confidence is legally defensible or there is a legal obligation to disclose confidential information.

Defensible breaches of confidence

The legal obligation to maintain confidentiality is not founded on protecting the interest of an individual merely because that individual considers that interest to be important. To base confidentiality on unilateral stipulations of importance would severely restrict the court's ability to consider wider issues. Judges will protect confidences where there are powerful public, as well as private, interests served by protecting it (Feldman, 1993: 435). Conversely, it has been established that a legal defence to breach of confidentiality will be granted where the balance of public interest is in favour of disclosure. A breach of confidence is defensible in the following circumstances.

(a) The client has consented to disclosure

For counsellors, obtaining the client's consent is often the best way of resolving legal and ethical dilemmas about confidentiality (Cohen, 1992: 19). A client's consent to disclosure is a recognition that the counsellor is no longer under an obligation to keep a confidence[10] (Kennedy and Grubb, 1994: 644). Legal consent may be explicit or implied. Because of the importance of confidentiality the codes of ethics and practice published by BAC require explicit consent in circumstances where other professions may regard implicit consent as adequate. For example, in health care it is usually considered adequate to assume consent for information to be shared within a multidisciplinary team in order for different team members to perform their task. In contrast, the current code for counsellors requires explicit consent (BAC, 1997: B.1.3.7).

(b) The confidences disclosed are already public knowledge

This defence is problematic for counsellors. Counsellors may have difficulty distinguishing information which is known to several people with each bound by confidentiality, and that which is so widely known that it can be considered public knowledge. Even when something is clearly a matter of public knowledge, counsellors may prefer to remain silent rather than run the risk of being seen by clients as someone who is unable to keep secrets.

(c) The balance between the public interest in the maintenance of confidentiality is outweighed by the public interest in disclosure

The term 'public interest' could be misleading. These are matters which are for the 'public good' rather than something which would interest the public if, for example, they were published in a newspaper. This defence poses many challenges for the counsellor or anyone else who wishes to rely upon it. Firstly, it requires balancing two opposing evaluations of public interest about confidentiality and disclosure. Neither of these can be precisely quantified and must involve a degree of personal opinion. Extreme situations are usually easier to decide. For example, it is clear that there is a greater public interest in preventing someone from poisoning the water supply to a community than in keeping confidentiality. On the balance of public interest, the courts have upheld that it was defensible for a psychiatrist to breach confidence in order to warn the authorities about a serious threat to public safety posed by a patient[11]. In some situations, where the balance is less easily weighed, it is possible that different counsellors faced with the same situation would come to different conclusions. It is probable that the court will be influenced by the care with which the decision has been made. Being able to demonstrate that the decision was made and implemented conscientiously is important. A court is likely to be interested in a number of issues:

i.   Has the counsellor acted in accordance with published codes and guidelines? The current BAC *Code of Ethics and Practice for Counsellors* is very relevant. B.3.4.1 requires that whenever possible any decision to breach confidentiality without a client's consent 'should be made only after consultation with a counselling supervisor or if he/she is not available an experienced counsellor'. Other guidelines may also apply to the specific situation e.g. agency policy statements, other professional codes etc.

ii. Have the disclosures been restricted to matters which are directly relevant to the reasons for disclosure? For example, a disclosure about someone's current state of mind and the danger that may be posed is appropriate. Detailed disclosures about current relationships or early childhood difficulties would be inappropriate unless they were considered to be directly relevant.

iii. Have any disclosures been restricted to people best able to act in the public interest? Who may properly be informed will vary according to the circumstances. Knowledge of local services is often invaluable in being able to identify people and organisations best able to respond. In some cases it may be most appropriate to warn a potential victim. All disclosures should be made on a confidential basis. In most circumstances, it would be difficult to justify disclosures to the press.

iv. Has the client been properly informed about the breach of confidence? The code for counsellors establishes a general principle that clients ought to have prior notice of circumstances in which confidentiality might be breached. It would be consistent with the fiduciary relationship to ensure that whenever possible a counsellor informed a client that she was considering breaking confidentiality. This would enable a discussion about the client's wishes. It is possible that the client will choose to disclose for himself. This is always the most preferred option because counsellors do not normally act on behalf of their clients (B.1.3.5) and is most respectful of client autonomy. If the client is unable or unwilling to act for himself, the next best option is acting with the client's consent. It respects the relationship of trust to inform clients about what has transpired during the disclosure. Sometimes it is impossible to forewarn clients of your intention to disclose confidential information, perhaps because they are too disturbed, or cannot be contacted. Good practice suggests that clients should be informed of any disclosure as soon as possible after it has been made.

(d) Crime

A counsellor cannot be legally bound to confidentiality about a crime. Courts have treated confidentiality about crime as an aspect of the public interest defence and have concluded that it is defensible to breach confidence, in good faith, in order to assist the prevention or detection of a crime. Good faith requires honesty and reasonable grounds for suspecting or knowing about a crime. However, there is no general duty to report crime except in specific circumstances – see statutory obligations below. There is also no general obligation to answer police questions about a client. A polite refusal on the grounds of confidentiality is sufficient if this is considered appropriate. (See later for statutory exceptions.) Giving misleading information or lying is likely to constitute an offence.

S115 Crime and Public Disorder Act 1998 enables people, who might not otherwise have the power, to pass confidential information between agencies in order to protect vulnerable communities from crime and disorder. The aim of the legislation is to promote confident and effective information exchange between agencies in order to develop inter-agency policy and joint strategies. Home Office guidelines envisage that the information that is exchanged routinely will not be about identifiable people. However, personally identifiable information would also be covered where this is consistent with the Act. Counselling agencies working with addicts or offenders should see Home Office guidelines. The legislation creates a power to disclose but does not impose a duty.

(e)   Counselling-supervision, training and research

Technically, it is a breach of confidence when counsellors discuss cases in counselling-supervision, training and research. It is best practice to obtain the client's consent. Even if this has not been obtained, the public interest in the proper training and supervision of counsellors, and in the development of a professional body of knowledge probably out-weighs the public interest in confidentiality to the extent of making defensible discussions which protect the identity of clients (Cohen. 1992: 22).

(f)   Suicidal clients

Responding appropriately to suicidal clients creates one of the most challenging situations encountered by counsellors. The management of confidentiality is inextricably linked to decisions about when to act in order to attempt to preserve life and when to remain silent out of respect for a client's autonomy. The situation is complicated because counsellors are not agreed amongst themselves about which approach should predominate (see B.3.4.3 in Code for Counsellors).

A counsellor who adheres strongly to one view or the other is advised to make that information available in pre-counselling information or to build in an appropriate agree-ment in the counselling contract. As there is no general duty to rescue in British law (Menlowe and McCall Smith, 1993), counsellors seeing fee-paying clients need to be explicit about reserving the power to breach confidentiality for a suicidal adult client. To do so without an explicit agreement may constitute an actionable breach of confidence. Reserving the power to breach confidentiality does not necessarily mean that the counsel-lor must notify in every instance of suicidal intent. (For consideration of criteria for assess-ment of suicidal risk see Bond, 1993: 84–5.)

Obligations to disclose which override confidentiality

Whenever there is a legal obligation to break confidentiality, the law also protects the counsellor from liability for that breach. Such an obligation can arise by:

(a)   Statutory law requiring disclosure

Some examples include the Prevention of Terrorism Act (Temporary Provisions) Act 1989, (s.18), which requires disclosure of information to assist the prevention or investi-gation of an act of terrorism connected with the affairs of Northern Ireland. Under S.27, the Drug Trafficking Offences Act 1986 (as amended by the Criminal Justice Act 1993) requires that a person must disclose to a constable as soon as reasonably practicable, if they know or suspect a person is concealing money made through drug trafficking and this information came to them in the course of their trade, profession, business or employment. Not to make this disclosure is an offence. The provisions of these two acts are severe limi-tations on civil liberties, indicating the government's view of the danger that they are designed to avert. To inform a client that you have notified the police could constitute a separate offence.

The Children Act 1989 (S.47) requires local authorities (i.e. social services) to investi-gate allegations of child abuse. It also imposes a qualified duty on workers in local authori-ties, local education authorities, local housing authorities, health authorities and others authorised by the Secretary of State to assist inquiries into child welfare by providing relevant information and advice except 'where doing so would be unreasonable in all the circumstances of the case' (s.47) (10). There is some uncertainty about the interpretation of this exception.

The Road Traffic Act 1988 (s.172) requires any person, upon request by a police officer, to provide information, which is in their power to supply, to permit identification of the driver of a motor vehicle involved in an offence. A doctor refused to answer oral and written requests from the police and was fined £5 in 1973, but never gave the information. On appeal it was held that a duty of confidence was insufficient to override the duties imposed by statute[12].

(b) Court orders

A court may require a counsellor to appear as a witness, with/without any records and require answers to questions regardless of breach of confidence. In actual practice, courts are sensitive to the ethical dilemma this poses for the counsellor. It is permissible as a 'conscientious witness' to request the court to waive or restrict its powers to order disclosure. This is probably best done through a barrister or solicitor. There are examples where the courts have accepted such a request (Hayman, 1965).

Counselling ethics require that confidentiality continues beyond the client's death. Therefore, counsellors who appear in the Coroners Court as witnesses to the cause of death (e.g. following a possible suicide) may face an ethical dilemma. It is a matter of professional judgement when to request the court's discretion in protecting confidences. This can often be resolved by discussion with the Coroner prior to the court appearance.

A client may request that a counsellor writes a report (which can be refused) or that a counsellor appears as a witness with any records in order to support their claim for emotional harm following a car accident or other claims. The counsellor is not obliged to act on the basis of such a request unless the counsellor is subject to a witness summons or subpoenaed (Jakobi and Pratt, 1992). However the counsellor has little option but to comply after being summoned or subpoenaed (Bond, 1993: 172).

(c) Recent developments

Examples of situations where counselling records may be sought by either the police or the courts appear to be increasing. Two of these have created ethical dilemmas for counsellors.

Firstly, courts under powers given to them by the Children Act 1989 have ordered the production of documents including personal medical reports which would otherwise have been protected from disclosure[13]. It has also been held that no privilege is attached to video recordings of therapy in which a child made allegations of abuse against her parents. This meant that the tapes had to be produced but the court restricted who was able to see them[14]. Courts exercise considerable investigative powers in many situations in which they are trying to determine the best interests of the child.

Secondly, the police acting on behalf of the Crown Prosecution Service and usually with the written consent of the client, may seek access to therapy and counselling notes. This is most likely to happen if they contain reports of allegations of rape or sexual abuse. This practice is problematic to counsellors because there is doubt about:

i   the quality of the client's consent as refusal would almost certainly result in the case being dropped;
ii the records will have been made from a therapeutic perspective which may not distinguish objective facts from subjective experience; and
iii the courts tend to view any factual changes in the client's account as evidence of the unreliability of the allegations rather than as evidence of rape trauma causing partial and progressive recall which would be a counselling interpretation.

The courts and Crown Prosecution Service consider that any objections to current practice are outweighed by the difficulty of judging rape trials and that the court should have all known sources of information made available to it including counselling notes, particularly if these contain the first allegation of rape or sexual assault. This is a situation where the counsellor may consider it appropriate to request that a judge reviews the notes and only releases those parts directly relevant to the case.

Conclusion

This information sheet outlines the law on confidentiality as it has affected counsellors over the last few years. It is not a comprehensive or definitive statement about the law but is based on an analysis of the best available information. Anyone with current concerns about confidentiality is encouraged to seek legal advice. Legal references have been included to assist the interested counsellor or her advisors.

Tim Bond
Senior Lecturer in Counselling
University of Bristol

References

Bainham, A. (1993) *Children: The Modern Law*. Bristol: Family Law.

Bollas, C. and Sundelson, D. (1995) *The New Informants: Betrayal of Confidentiality in Psychoanalysis and Psychotherapy*. London: Karnac.

Bond, T. (1993) S*tandards and Ethics for Counselling in Action*. London: Sage.

British Association for Counselling (1997) *Code of Ethics and Practice for Counsellors*. Rugby: BAC.

Children's Legal Centre (1997) *Offering Children Confidentiality: Law and Guidance*. University of Essex: CLC.

Cohen, K. (1992) Some legal issues in counselling and psychotherapy. *British Journal of Guidance and Counselling*, 20(1): 10–25.

Curry, F. (1985) *Breach of Confidence*. Oxford: Clarendon Press.

Feldman, D. (1993) *Civil Liberties and Human Rights in England and Wales*. Oxford: Clarendon Press.

Friel, J. (1992) In the matter of the powers of Her Majesty's Inspector of Schools to inspect counselling in polytechnics, colleges of further education etc. Unpublished legal opinion obtained by the British Association for Counselling.

Friel, J. (1998) In the matter of the British Association for Counselling, the Association for Student Counselling and the Association of Colleges. Unpublished legal opinion obtained by the British Association for Counselling.

Hayman, A. (First published anonymously) (1965) Psychoanalyst subpoenaed. *The Lancet*, 16 October: 785–6.

Human Fertilisation and Embryology Authority (1993) *Code of Practice*. London: HFEA.

Jakobi, S. and Pratt, D. (1992) Therapy notes and the law. *The Psychologist*, May: 219–21.

Jenkins, P. (1997) *Counselling, Psychotherapy and the Law*. London: Sage.

Kennedy, I. and Grubb, A. (1994) *Medical Law: Text with Materials*. London: Butterworth.

Law Commission (1981) *Breach of Confidence*. London: HMSO Cmnd 8388.

Menlowe, M. and McCall Smith, A. (editors) (1993) *The Duty to Rescue: Jurisprudence of AID*. Aldershot: Dartmouth Pub. Co.

Rutherford, L. and Bone, S. (1993) *Osborn's Concise Law Dictionary* (Eighth Edition). London: Sweet and Maxwell.

Standing Conference on Drug Abuse (1994) *Building Confidence: Advice for Alcohol and Drugs Services on Confidentiality Policies*. London: SCODA/Alcohol Concern.

Wacks, R. (1989) *Personal Information: Privacy and the Law*. Oxford: Clarendon Press.

Cases

1   Prince Albert v Strange (1849) 2 De Gex and Sm. 652 (on appeal) 1 Mac and G 25; Margaret, Duchess of Argyll v Duke of Argyll [1967] 1 Ch 302 [1965] 1 All ER 611.
2   Coco v A.N. Clark (Engineers) Ltd. [1969] RPC 41.
3   Hunter v Mann [1974] QB 767 at 722 per Boreham J.; X v Y [1988] 2 All ER 648 and W v Egdell [1990] 1 All ER 835, (1989) 4 BLMR 96 (CA).
4   Attorney General v Guardian Newspapers (No. 2) [1988] 3 All ER 545 at 658 per Lord Goff.
5   Duncan v Medical Practitioners' Disciplinary Committee (1986) NZLR, p. 513 per Jeffries J.
6   Gillick v West Norfolk Area Health Authority [1985] 3 All ER 402, HL.
7   Under 16 year olds: Re. R [1992] 1FLR 190.
8   16–18 year olds: Re. W (A Minor) (Medical Treatment: Courts Jurisdiction) [1992] 3 WLR 758.
9   X v Y [1988] 2 All ER 648.
10   Fraser v Thames Television Ltd. [1983] 2 All ER 101 at 122 per Hirst J.
11   W v Egdell [1990] 1 All ER 835, (1989) 4 BLMR 96 (CA).
12   Hunter v Mann [1974] QB 767.
13   Oxfordshire County Council v M, *The Times*, 2 November 1993, CA.
14   B v B (Child abuse: evidence) [1991] 2 FLR 487.

British Association for
Counselling and **Psychotherapy**

1 Regent Place
Rugby
Warwickshire CV21 2PJ
Office: 01788 550899
Information Line: 01788 578328
Fax 01788 562189
Minicom: 01788 572838
email: bac@bac.co.uk
http://www.counselling.co.uk
Company limited by guarantee 2175320 • registered in England & Wales • Registered Charity 298361

Appendix B

Confidentiality Guidelines for College Counsellors
in Further Education and Sixth Form Colleges

1   These guidelines have been produced on the basis of information obtained from a legal opinion concerning confidentiality for counsellors in FE commissioned by the British Association for Counselling (1997), Circular 10/95 Protecting Children from Abuse: The Role of the Education Service (DFEE,) 1995 and Working Together to Safeguard Children (Department of Health, Home Office and DFEE, 1999). They take into account that further education and sixth form colleges have been brought within the scope of sections 27 and 47 of the Children Act 1989 by the Secretary of State.

2   The first point to appreciate is that there are three potential classes of students with whom counsellors may be called upon to advise and where there may be a potential for conflict between the confidentiality of the discussions with the student and the college's desire of disclosure:

    a)   young people under 16
    b)   students between 16–18
    c)   students over the age of 18

3   The first category of students even though under the age of 16 may be 'Gillick' competent i.e. of sufficient age and understanding that they may be treated for all intents and purposes as if they were 16. The third category does not fall within the scope of this advice which is primarily concerned with students in the middle category.

4   The legal opinion obtained by BACP emphasises that a counsellor has a common law obligation to maintain confidentiality. 'Colleges are not in a position to impose disclosure as they appear to be doing in practice. In doing so they are going over the line' drawn by law in this situation. In all circumstances an element of professional judgement by the counsellor must be involved. 'Contractual arrangements which go beyond this are clearly vulnerable to challenge both in judicial review and indeed private law claims.'

5   Clients over the age of 18 should be treated as adults with regard to their legal rights to confidentiality and must normally consent to any disclosures of personally sensitive information. Young people under the age of 18 should be assessed and those of sufficient intelligence and understanding, and therefore competent to give appropriate instructions, are entitled to the same level of confidentiality as adults.

6   Good practice has been undermined by a number of widely held false beliefs about the law and current policy. The law corrects these misapprehensions. A college's legal responsibilities of standing in loco parentis for under 18 year olds does not override the counsellor's responsibility to exercise professional judgement in the management of confidences. The Children Act 1989 does not create a general legal obligation to disclose all suspicion of abuse. In correspondence with the Association of University and College Counsellors, a Division of BACP, the Department of Education and Employment have appreciated that counsellors are in a different position from teachers and lecturers.

7　When counsellors receive information from clients concerning the abuse of children and young people under 18 years of age they have the challenging task of deciding how best to protect the young people concerned, including any other young people at risk from the same abuser, whilst working in a relationship with the client in which trust and confidentiality are fundamental. These are professionally challenging decisions which can only be made with up to date information on best practice, adequate training, readily available professional supervision and support and the opportunity to form constructive professional relationships with other agencies involved with child protection or members of the Area Child Protection Committee. It is strongly recommended that a counsellor seeks advice from BACP if they are unsure as to the appropriate action to take.

8　As trust and confidentiality are so fundamental to counselling, best practice requires that counsellors seek the consent of their clients for any disclosure of personally sensitive information. The client must also be given adequate information and time to make a considered decision. Some circumstances may override the conscientious endeavour to seek a client's consent, particularly the urgency of the situation, the seriousness of the impending harm to the client or others, the client's lack of sufficient understanding to give consent, or where seeking the client's consent would expose the client to greater harm. Forewarning the client of any limitations to confidentiality in advance of counselling is considered good practice but is insufficient by itself to authorise automatic disclosure. It is still necessary to give serious consideration to obtaining the client's consent to specific disclosures and involving the client in decisions about how the disclosure should be made. Sometimes the counsellor's role will be to support clients in making the disclosure for themselves and assisting them through any consequences of that disclosure.

9　The provisions of the Children Act 1989 create a legal distinction between circumstances in which the counsellor has greater or lesser scope to exercise professional judgement. The distinction depends on whether or not the counsellor is responding to an inquiry made by the local authority under section 47.

10　An inquiry made under section 47 of the Children Act 1989 by the local authority requires the college, and therefore any directly involved counsellors, to assist that authority where there are reasonable grounds to suspect that a child or young person is suffering or likely to suffer significant harm.

　　This obligation requires offering information and advice. The Children Act qualifies this obligation by exempting any person from assisting 'where doing so would be unreasonable in all the circumstances of the case' (s47 (11)). Working Together (1999) directs the local authority, usually the social services department, undertaking the inquiry to be clear 'about whether the consent of the subject of the information requested has been obtained or whether in the view of social services, such consent-seeking would itself place a child at risk of significant harm'. (p 14: 3.7). This guidance will greatly assist counsellors and others in making professional judgements. Counsellors are recommended to draw the guidance to people's attention and to seek to have it incorporated into any local or institutional guidelines.

11　The majority of counsellors' concerns about abuse to children and young people arise in circumstances about which the local authority has not made any inquiry and the counsellor is deciding whether to take the initiative in communicating his/her concern. Circular 10/95 and Working Together (1999) require that all colleges produce Guidelines for Reporting Abuse. These guidelines would be an important source of guidance in deciding how to respond to a client's specific circumstances. It is recommended that a college counsellor should be involved in writing these and participate in any committee established to oversee the functioning of such guidance.

12　A particularly challenging situation arises when a client tells a counsellor about a risk to children posed by someone else. Often the counsellor will have no direct knowledge of either the children or the alleged abuser. Again there is no general legal obligation for the counsellor to inform the authorities The counsellor's role will more usually be to support the client in contacting the authorities. Sometimes a client may be reluctant to inform about seemingly well-founded concerns because of fear about becoming identified as the informant. It may be appropriate to consider whether they would prefer to inform the National Society for the Protection of Children (or similar organisation) who are usually better placed legally to protect the identity of the informer than the statutory agencies. In some situations (such as identified in paragraph 8) the counsellor would be justified in directly informing the NSPCC or the authorities after taking all the circumstances into consideration.

13   It is now generally accepted that professional collaboration and co-operation between workers and agencies is fundamental to successful strategies to protect young people from abuse. These guidelines are intended to support this policy and to enable its implementation in ways that are consistent with good professional practice in counselling.

14   For counsellors who are unsure what action to take in a particular set of circumstances, BACP offers a professional information and advice service on these and other matters.

The publication of these Guidelines is in response to concerns raised by AUCC and has been greatly assisted by Jill Collins of AUCC and by Alan Jamieson, BACP Deputy Chief Executive. BACP commissioned legal opinion and requested Dr Tim Bond, Reader in Counselling and Professional Ethics, University of Bristol, to prepare these Guidelines.

British Association for
Counselling and **Psychotherapy**

1 Regent Place
Rugby
Warwickshire CV21 2PJ
Office: 01788 550899
Information Line: 01788 578328
Fax 01788 562189
Minicom: 01788 572838
email: bac@bac.co.uk
http://www.counselling.co.uk
Company limited by guarantee 2175320 • registered in England & Wales • Registered Charity 298361

Appendix C

Guidelines for University and College Counselling Services 1998 (an extract)

Working with disturbed and disturbing students

To define exactly what we mean by *disturbed* is difficult. It is important to distinguish between that behaviour which is rebellious and challenging within an institution and that which is a result of serious and emotional disorder. This latter disturbance may not be easily contained by an institution and may result in threat or damage to self or others.

Examples that have come to our attention:

- A student being allowed to stay at college by a disciplinary committee, providing that s/he is seen regularly by the counsellor.
- Expectation of the institution that the Counselling Service should see a severely disturbed student with an extreme psychiatric history.
- Expectation of a college that an aggressive confrontation between a student and tutor should be resolved by a counsellor.
- Requests from a student already being treated by local psychiatric services for alternative help from the Counselling Service.

This section is particularly concerned with those students who arrive at counselling services inappropriately, either through self-referral or through referral by staff within the institution. Counselling services need to have clear codes of practice to assist them in correct assessment and matching of client needs with the resource. Likewise they need to be able to help their institutions in the development of college-wide policy.

Relationship within the institution

Disturbed students will be experienced as difficult by the whole institution as well as the counsellor. The institution may look to the Counselling Service for help. This request may be made more in the way of inappropriate referrals than through discussion (BACP Code of Ethics and Practice for Counsellors B.6.1.2 and 6.1.4 – referred to hereafter as 'Code').

Reasonable expectations of the institution
- Professional concern from the Counselling Service including a willingness to pool knowledge and experience (Code B.1.5).
- That the Counselling Service will contribute to the development of policy.
- A willingness to contribute to the institution's understanding of its boundaries and limitations, e.g. some students will be too difficult to contain in a college. This contribution might include training for staff.
- That the Counselling Service will provide information about other agencies and services and be active in arranging referrals where appropriate.

- A willingness to offer support to staff or students who may themselves have been distressed by violent or bizarre incidents.

Unreasonable expectations of the counsellor
- Responsibility for seeing students who are difficult for the institution but have not sought the counsellor's help. This is a clear management responsibility.
- That s/he be involved in a disciplinary or security crisis intervention role.
- Being expected to accompany students in medical emergency situations (Code B.4.3.3 and 5.1).
- That s/he be expected to give a diagnostic assessment of a student's behaviour which may be used by the institution against the student. Management must gain this information from the appropriate speciality, e.g. psychiatry, social work, legal professionals and police (Code B.1.3.1, 4.3.3, 1.6.3, 4.3.1, 4.3.2 and 6.1.7).

Code of practice within the counselling service

A clear code of practice agreed within the Counselling Service and supported by the institution will allow for a more confident response to and assessment of students who should be seen elsewhere.

Questions to help the appropriate assessment of a client
- Has the client chosen to come to the Counselling Service either through self-referral or agreed through a third party? (Code B.4.3.2.)
- Does the client have realistic expectations of what the Counselling Service Offers? (Code B.4.3.1 and 4.3.2.)
- Is there any previous or current psychiatric or medical history which might contra-indicate counselling?
- Are the capacity and resources able to match the need, i.e. expertise and training of counsellors, limitations of time and space available, proximity to the end of the course, long breaks, etc? (Code A.6 and B.6.1.2 and 6.1.4.)
- What are the client support networks?

Professional links

- Is there any easy access to local medical and psychiatric services for consultation and referral? Appropriate professional liaison needs to be not only developed but maintained between other agencies who may be referral points a Counselling Service.
- Does the institution recognise BACP's Codes of Ethics and Practice? Institutions can effect this through organisational membership of BACP and through incorporation of the Code into Health & Safety Policy.
- Are there any clear channels for discussion and exchange of information with management, e.g. discussion on referral policies?
- Is there any opportunity within the supervisory relationship to focus on institutional dynamics as well as individual casework?

Conclusion

The population of our colleges is increasingly diverse and the traditional pastoral support available is becoming diluted or disappearing. Diminishing support structures lead to increasing pressures on counselling services.

In this climate, with greater numbers and less personal support, the disturbed student can provoke much anxiety which may be passed on to the counselling service to be handled. This sometimes inappropriate displacement of anxiety can be difficult to resist.

It is hoped that this section will assist counsellors and counselling services to think through their own internal practices as well as the relationship with the institution as a whole in order that negotiations with management can be held with more confidence.

This section should be read in conjunction with the BACP Code of Ethics & Practice for Counsellors 1 January 1998.

AUCC Association for University and College Counselling

Appendix D

Bullying and Harassment: Policy and Guidelines

Bullying and harassment are issues which can deeply affect the lives of pupils, family and staff. They can create an atmosphere of intimidation. As members of the school community, we all have a role in reporting incidents of bullying and harassment. This policy and guidelines may overlap with other school policies, including the anti-racist multicultural and sexual equality policies, and policies and guidelines that are being put together on child protection. There is therefore some cross-referencing to pick up on relevant procedures elsewhere. It is important that on this whole range of difficult issues, staff are trained to provide a level of support to others and to deal with situations appropriately.

Schools nowadays are required to have policies relating to bullying and it is important to develop a clear policy. It is also an issue which is very difficult for teachers and others to confront and deal with. Therefore an important part of this document has been to develop guidelines about how to cope with this problem. The strategies suggested are not intended to be exhaustive, but may be helpful, particularly to tutors and other staff involved.

It is important for us to be sensitive to the fact that victims may be afraid to come forward, may insist on confidentiality and be unwilling to identify those who are at the source of their misery. It is important too that we respect a pupil's right to confidentiality, though this should not prevent staff seeking the support of other colleagues. Indeed, this should be encouraged. Confidentiality, of course, is different, in the case of the counselling services.

Bullying and harassment can take many forms, but for the sake of simplicity and clarity, this policy and its associated guidelines is confined to dealing with bullying among pupils, although it could involve those who are not pupils at the school.

Policy

Bullying and harassment are totally unacceptable and the school is committed to the eradication of all such forms of behaviour. In every instance where there are allegations of bullying/harassment:

- they will be investigated as speedily as possible;
- there will be feedback to the victim (where known) and reports of such incidents within five working days;
- support will be available for victims of such behaviour through the personal tutor and the counselling service;
- action will be taken to minimise the chances of recurrence where possible;
- firm measures will be taken against the perpetrators of such behaviour, if necessary leading to their exclusion from the school.

What is bullying?

Bullying occurs where an individual or group seeks to intimidate or persecute another through their perceived or actual strength or power. It could involve (but does not always involve) the use of threat of physical violence. It can involve:

- actual or threatened physical violence;
- verbal abuse or intimidation;
- written abuse or threats, including graffiti;
- name calling and teasing, sometimes of a racist, sexist or sexual nature;
- blackmail or other forms of extortion, including theft of student's work;
- exclusion for no good reason.

Because bullying often involves subtle threats and innuendo, it may not always be immediately apparent or explicit. It can often involve the deliberate isolation of individuals, so that they feel lonely, friendless and with nowhere to go. It can occur over a short, transitory period, or go on for very long periods of time.

Procedures

Action is always required when bullying or harassment is alleged, or where a member of staff witnesses an incident involving bullying/harassment. This does not necessarily involve rushing around trying to solve the problem. The following course of action, however, is required.

When bullying/harassment in alleged

1   Establish the importance of confidentiality, while at the same time indicating what support is available should the victim make allegations which would identify them.
2   Establish what happened and record the events as presented.
3   Reinforce the fact that the school views bullying/harassment as unacceptable.
4   Encourage the victim(s) to divulge the identity of the perpetrators.
5   Immediately notify the headteacher, depending on the severity of the incident.
6   Arrangements should be made to interview the alleged perpetrators and any witnesses as soon as possible, by the headteacher and/or the deputy head, as appropriate.
7   The appropriate form of the Discipline Procedure should be applied. In cases where there is proven violence or threats of violence, this should be treated as gross misbehaviour and the pupil excluded from school as a consequence.
8   Parents must be informed.

When an incident involving bullying/harassment is witnessed

1   If necessary and if possible, call on the support of colleagues. In the case of inflammatory situations or those involving violence or threatened violence, seek the support of the headteacher (in which case, they will perform the tasks which follow).
2   Attempt to identify those present, including any witnesses.
3   Deal with each of those involved separately, if at all possible.
4   Separate the victim(s) and perpetrator(s) if at all possible.
5   Take signed statements from those involved.
6   Draw up a signed statement of what you witnessed.
7   The appropriate form of the Discipline Procedure should be applied. In cases where there is proven violence or threats of violence, this should be treated as Gross Misbehaviour and the pupil excluded from the school as a consequence.

It is important in cases where there is alleged racism or sexism within a bullying/harassment context, that the appropriate school procedures are adhered to.

Guidelines on dealing with cases of bullying/harassment

Victims of bullying/harassment may feel:

- isolated
- frightened
- humiliated and lacking in self-worth (because they cannot stand up to the bully or because they think something is lacking in their own personality)
- depressed, trapped or even suicidal.

Victims may need *physical protection* (especially where there is a perceived threat of violence or aggressive behaviour).

1 This may have a bearing on how the perpetrators are dealt with (see below).
2 Every step should be taken to minimise physical risks.
3 It should be pointed out to the perpetrators, if possible, that physical assault is a criminal offence.

Victims may need to talk and be listened to/counselling.

1 Victims' feelings may get in the way of their willingness to talk, i.e. if they feel humiliated or lacking in self-worth, they may find it difficult to acknowledge the problem so openly.
2 Victims can be encouraged to use the counselling service.
3 Parents should be briefed and consulted.
4 Every opportunity should be given to the victim to talk in confidence about their difficulties.
5 For many victims, the first instinct may be to escape by leaving school, or absenting themselves for long periods. While this is understandable, the victim should be encouraged to come back to school and to work through the issues.

Dealing with perpetrators

1 They should be dealt with separately. The fact that there is more than one of them is inherent in many bullying situations and therefore they should be discouraged from associating with one another on school premises (although in practice, this may be difficult to enforce).
2 Every opportunity should be made to make it clear that bullying and harassment are unacceptable.
3 If they are to continue as pupils at the school, the consequences of continuing the same pattern of behaviour should be clearly stated.
4 If relevant, it should be clearly pointed out to the perpetrators that physical assault is a criminal offence, and that the school would seek to involve the police in such an eventuality.
5 Perpetrators should be asked searching questions about their motivation in bullying/harassment and how they would feel as a victim. Many bullies do not realise that what they are doing constitutes bullying, do not acknowledge their own role and fail to see the traumatic consequences for the victim.

6 The personal tutor should be briefed at the earliest opportunity.
7 Perpetrators should be encouraged to meet with the personal tutor/course leader individually over a period of time on an ongoing basis, in order to work through issues relating to bullying. The counselling service can also be involved in this process.

The role of the personal tutor

The role of the tutor is important in a number of ways:

1 Dealing with the issues of bullying and harassment is an important element in educating pupils about relationships, and sensitising them to an awareness of their effect on other people and the feelings of others.
2 The issues of bullying and harassment should be dealt with at a relatively early stage in tutor groups. Supportive materials should be available for personal tutors to use. Many pupils have vivid memories and experiences of bullying and harassment and these should be drawn upon sensitively during tutorials and during these sessions. Dealing with these issues at an early stage can have a pre-emptive effect in reducing incidents involving bullying.
3 The personal tutor has a crucial role to play where incidents of bullying and harassment take place (see above). They may have an ongoing role in using such incidents sensitively in the social education of young people.
4 Because bullying can have such a profound effect on the victim, they may well require a great deal of ongoing support. Personal tutors may well need support from the school counsellor in meeting this requirement.
5 Victims of bullying need to know what the options are for their given situation.
6 Incidents of bullying need to be recorded.

Appendix E

Genogram Symbols

□	Male	⊡	Carriers of sex-linked or recessive genes
○	Female		
⊠	Death	□—○ 1975	Marriage and year
●	Spontaneous abortion	□—○ 1994	Divorce and year
ȯ	Induced abortion		
△	Pregnancy	□—○ 1982	Separation and year
⚭⚭	Dyzigotic twins		
⚭⚭	Monozygotic twins	□ ○ 1975	Not married, year started living together
A □	Adopted	∿∿∿	Conflictual relationship
		....	Distant relationship
'88 □ John	Year of birth Name	═══	Close relationship
⊠ 78	Age at death	══	Overly close relationship
'66–'96 ⊠ CA	Year of birth and death Cause of death	⟶	Dominant relationship
		□∿∿○	Marital discord
□—○ 1986 ○ ○ ○	Solid or dashed line indicates individuals living together	□—□	Same sex couple

Basic genogram symbols

Appendix F

Access to Records of Counselling and Psychotherapy

1 General principles governing access to records

The need to respect client confidentiality is a core principle of counselling and psychotherapy training and practice, underpinned by a wider ethical commitment to promoting the client's personal development and potential for autonomy. The importance of maintaining client confidentiality is endorsed by the law in three main ways:

Duty of confidence to client

Therapists owe a duty of confidence to the client because of the special nature of the relationship, where maintaining the trust and privacy of personal information is a legitimate expectation for the client. Confidentiality can also be protected by the specific terms of a legally binding contract. The law sets great store on confidentiality, although counselling confidentiality does not possess the kind of legal protection or 'privilege' associated with situations where a client is seeking legal advice from a solicitor. The concept of legal privilege is, in brief, the right of confidentiality held by the client of a solicitor when in contact with a solicitor for the purposes of obtaining legal advice. The client cannot be forced by law to reveal information about the legal advice sought, nor be made to give evidence about such advice in court. The right of privilege is held by the client, not the solicitor. It can, therefore, generally only be waived by the decision of the client.

Public interest versus counselling confidentiality

Ultimately therapeutic confidentiality, however vital a principle, is decisively outweighed by the concept of the 'public interest'. The public interest, i.e. what is seen to be good for society as a whole, is ultimately defined by Acts of Parliament and by decisions of the courts. Hence disclosing confidential client information may be carried out in the public interest where therapists decide, for example, to report child abuse, serious crime or threatened harm to a third party.

The needs of the justice system

The public interest also lies in the justice system having the fullest possible access to information or material relevant to hearing cases in a proper and fair manner. The courts can, therefore, override the therapist's duty of confidentiality where the needs of justice require that client information is made available to the legal system. This may happen, for example, in a civil case where a client is suing another person for damages or in a criminal trial.

The needs of the justice system affect record keeping practice in a number of ways via:

- the process of 'discovery' of documents in civil and criminal proceedings
- potential for access to original notes made of therapy
- a requirement for a therapist to act as witness in a court case

It is important, therefore, for therapists to be fully aware of the wide range of external agencies or individuals who can gain access to the very sensitive personal information disclosed and explored in therapy. This is necessary to have a realistic grasp of the limits to any undertakings of confidentiality that can realistically be made to clients concerning the future uses of personal material disclosed in therapy. A first step to consider within systems of recording is to distinguish clearly between different types of information:

- directly observed fact
- opinion, based on professional training and experience
- personal, subjective and reflective material

Second sets of records and their 'ownership'

Records of therapy, in whatever form, represent a permanent source of information on the content and process of counselling and psychotherapy. This permanence means that it may continue to exist long after the actual therapeutic work has ended. It may be used in ways which the therapist, as author of the recordings, and the client, as its subject, can no longer easily control. Therapists may try to exercise control over external access to counselling records by a number of different methods. Factual records can be kept for the employing counselling organisation or agency, and more sensitive 'process' or 'personal notes' are often kept separately from the main client file, perhaps at the counsellor's home. One justification for this may be that, while the agency 'owns' the official file, the second set of notes is seen as the personal property of the therapist, who might be presumed to control their release or disclosure.

The flaws with this approach are, by now, well established. Second sets of notes are still part of the client's record in the eyes of the law, and are required to be disclosed if so ordered by the court. 'Ownership' of notes is also problematic. Notes on clients are, generally speaking, the property of the employing organisation. Notes kept by a therapist in private practice belong to that therapist, but may still need to be disclosed if ordered by the courts. Records kept by a self-employed therapist providing a service for a referring agency, such as an Employee Assistance Programme, can be designated as agency property under the terms of the contract existing between the agency and therapist.

Rights of the data subject

The professional culture within counselling and psychotherapy, whereby the practitioner keeps a record not designed for sharing with the client, is also under challenge from recent data protection law. The principle of extended rights of citizen's access to recorded information, with limited exceptions, is at the heart of the European Directive informing the Data Protection Act 1998. The therapist's assumption of a strong degree of protection for subjective recorded material is not supported by the cultural change towards much more open and transparent recording systems. Other professional groups such as, medicine, social work and teaching have now introduced these more accessible recording systems. While the recording of the therapist's subjective personal experience and perceptions of the therapy may present problematic issues for client access, therapists do not possess any privileged legal status which would limit or prevent client access to this material.

2   Access to counselling and psychotherapy records

Data Protection Act 1998

The primary means for clients to gain access to records of therapy will be via the Data Protection Act 1998 which qualifies earlier legislation on access to computerised files, and access to more specialist files held by health, social work and education agencies.

Computerised records

The Act, effective from March 2000, introduces client (or 'data subject') access in the broadest possible sense to computerised records. Individuals and agencies involved in processing data on living, identifiable individuals, must notify the Data Protection Registrar, and comply with specific data protection principles. These specify that information must be normally processed with client or data subject consent (explicit consent in the case of 'sensitive personal data', e.g. relating to emotional or physical health, sexual life). Personal data must be lawfully processed, accurate, not excessive, retained no longer than necessary, and kept under secure conditions.

Wordprocessed records

Personal data, which is processed purely for domestic purposes (e.g. a Xmas card list), does not require notification under the Act. This exemption also applies to personal data which is used solely for historical purposes, or for research, where the data processing will not cause substantial damage or distress to the data subject. Students using computers to wordprocess records as part of assignments, e.g. for the purpose of a training course, will normally be covered by the notification requirement applying to their educational institution. Apart from these specific exceptions, wordprocessing of personal data related to clients will presumably be considered to be data processing under the Act, requiring appropriate compliance with the data protection principles, including notification with the Data Protection Registrar.

Health records

Therapists involved in providing a service to clients as part of delegated care, under the overall direction of a health professional, such as a GP, may try to protect client confidentiality by keeping therapeutic records separately from medical notes, under secure conditions. Such therapeutic records would constitute part of the client's 'health record' for the purposes of data protection, governed by separate regulations (SI 2000 No. 413). The client or data subject could gain access to their therapy notes, as part of their health record, with certain provisos. Access to information identifying contributions by third parties, e.g. family members, may be withheld to protect the confidentiality of these third parties. Access to information may also be withheld where access would result in 'serious harm' being caused to the data subject, or to another person. Access to the files of a deceased client would be governed by the Access to Health Records Act 1990.

Accessible records

Other specialist records, i.e. social work and education files, are governed by similar regulations, with provision for restricting access to information on third parties, and where it would cause harm to the data subject or other persons.

Manual records

The Data Protection Act 1998 specifically includes certain manual records within its remit, which enables the data subject to gain access to his or her personal file. The criteria are that the file includes personal data on a living, identifiable individual, where the file is part of a 'relevant filing system'.

Relevant filing systems

This system enables specific information on identifiable, living individual data subjects to be readily accessed. Formats might include filing systems, card indexes, roneodexes, etc.

Unstructured data

Unsorted files not providing ready access to individual data would not therefore be counted as part of 'a relevant filing system'. Such files would not require notification with the Data Protection Registrar.

Audio and video recordings

Audio and video recordings, which are part of a relevant filing systems, are also covered by the provisions of the Act, and would be potentially accessible to the client.

Information on third parties

Client access to records in not an absolute right in law, but needs to be balanced against the rights of others, in particular the latter's right to confidentiality. In one case the courts have refused access to a client seeking information on his birth mother, on the grounds that it was clear in this situation that the client's violent history would place his birth mother at real risk of harm or worse. More usually, where a client's record contains letters, reports or documents from third parties, such as the original referring agent, then the consent of the latter needs to be sought before making disclosure to the client. Here again, whereas this used to be applied in a fairly rigid manner, the spirit of the data protection legislation had shifted away from blanket refusals of client access on the grounds of protecting third party confidentiality. Organisations faced with this dilemma need to have well thought-out policies indicating where disclosure of third party information can be made when it is impractical to obtain the latter's consent, perhaps because of the passage of time, or because of the lack of means of contacting the third party concerned.

Serious harm

In the limited case of health, education and social work records, client or data subject access can be denied where such access would cause the client or other party 'serious harm'. Serious harm relates to the physical or mental health or condition of the data subject or third party concerned. Previous case law in this area includes refusal of access on these grounds relating to sensitive information about child abuse allegations or information supplied by family members relating to a diagnosis of a major psychiatric disorder. Where the therapy record is part of a wider set of records kept by a health professional, as would be the case of a therapist working in primary care under the overall clinical responsibility of a GP, then the decision to permit client access to third party information rests with the appropriate health professional, rather than with the therapist alone. Information in the record on third party medical professionals can be accessed, but again not where this would result in serious harm arising to that health professional (SI 2000 No. 413).

Access to counselling and psychotherapy records by the police

Therapists are sometimes approached by the police for access to their records, in connection with ongoing investigations, perhaps into child abuse allegations. The police have no privileged access to therapeutic records without a warrant issued by a circuit judge. Under s.12, Police and Criminal Evidence Act 1984, counselling records are specifically excluded from police powers of search and seizure, unless authorised by a warrant. In a case heard at Cardiff Crown Court in 1993, the judge upheld the right of a psychiatrist to refuse the police access to medical records under this Act. The police had requested access to medical records of a local psychiatric unit in order to carry out investigation of a murder committed nearby. In this situation, the court was prepared to defend the confidential status of medical records against the police case for access (Kellam, 1994). This case may come to have a wide relevance should there be a similar case in the future involving court action by the police for access to records of therapy.

Access to counselling and psychotherapy records by solicitors

Solicitors show increasing interest in gaining access to therapeutic records for the purposes of assisting their client in legal action, or in building a case for compensation, for example for workplace stress.

Request for access to therapeutic records by a solicitor   A straightforward request by a solicitor for access to a client's counselling or psychotherapy records may be declined, however impressive the notepaper, and imperious the tone. As a first step, the client's consent to release of the records must be confirmed, for the therapist to avoid making a simple breach of confidentiality. Therapists and their organisations may opt for the policy of not releasing records, even with the client's consent, without a subpoena as part of a declared policy, in order to avoid being drawn unwittingly into legal proceedings.

Request for a written report by a solicitor or client   Either the client or their solicitor may request that the therapist prepare a report for use in court proceedings. Therapists are not usually trained in the preparation of such reports, and again may find their willingness to support the client in a course of action may have unintended consequences for themselves. A brief confirmation of the number of therapy sessions may seem appropriate for a client claiming compensation under the Criminal Injuries Compensation Scheme. Therapists involved in writing any report for the courts need to remind themselves constantly of the crucial distinction between describing directly observed fact, and in attempting to offer any professional opinion (or even recommendation) to the court.

Therapists who lack formal training in assessment procedures may well find their expertise seriously challenged in court if expressing professional opinions via a court report. It has also been the case that preparation of a court report enables the opposing legal representatives to request access to the original notes and records of therapy, including audio- and video-tapes where appropriate. Once involved in preparation of a report for court, therapists may become involved in progressively greater levels of disclosure of client records, well beyond that originally intended.

Access to counselling and psychotherapy records by the courts

Principle of the public interest versus counselling confidentiality   Counsellors and psychotherapists may feel bound by confidentiality under professional codes of ethics, but they do not possess privilege as such. In contrast, solicitors are protected against any requirement to reveal client information obtained in the process of the latter obtaining legal advice. According to one Judge, 'confidentiality is not a separate head of privilege', meaning that therapists cannot prevent court access to their records on the simple grounds that they are 'confidential'. The legal system operates on the basis of the public interest being served by the courts having the fullest possible access to evidential information required for resolving a case being decided.

Process of 'discovery'   The court's access to the widest range of information potentially relevant to hearing a court case is operated by the process of 'discovery'. Under this the court can authorise disclosure of therapy records to both sets of legal representatives, in civil and criminal proceedings. Therapists may feel that the release of their records will be against their client's interests. For example, very sensitive personal information about early childhood experiences or current marital problems, may be made accessible to the court, even though this is not relevant to deciding a court case over compensation for anxiety following a car crash. In situations such as this, one option is for the therapist or counselling organisation to make the case for limiting disclosure of the records to the Judge via a barrister, in a manner consistent with the appropriate protocols of the court.

3   Recording counselling and psychotherapy sessions

Purpose and function of records

The employing agency may require certain forms of recording, such as assessments, goals, outcomes achieved, etc. In addition, recordings often focus strongly on the therapeutic relationship, necessarily providing a subjective account of the process and experience. In many cases, counsellors keep a separate set of notes, i.e. an objective one for agency records, and a set of 'process notes' for the purposes of personal and professional development, training and supervision. The courts do not accept this distinction when operating the process of 'discovery'. This distinction may also be challenged by the principle of client access under data protection law. Under the Data Protection Act 1998, the crucial element is not the intended purpose of the counselling record (process notes as opposed to agency record). Data protection law is primarily concerned with the status and structure of the therapeutic record (i.e whether it is a computerised, structured or unstructured manual file), which may thus enable the client to have access to the record. It may be wise to assume that most files are in fact structured, in the absence of definitive case law. Practitioners may opt for keeping brief records, which are designed to be shared on a regular basis with clients. Therapists and their agencies may also wish to consider the possible benefits of 'active' or open systems of client access to records, rather than 'passive' systems, where client access is an unusual event, triggered only by the occasion of a direct request by a client.

Types of information

Therapists might consider it useful to adopt the following criteria for evaluating the content of their recording. Client information, which is recorded, may fall into the following categories, with the actual detail varying from one setting or client group to another.

Type of information:	Content of counselling and psychotherapy record:
Qualifying:	Employee/patient/student status, etc
Contextual:	Address, date of birth (if relevant)

Core:	Number of sessions attended; initial assessment information; outcomes if relevant
Critical:	Information with major and even life-and-death significance: Contact for GP; mobile phone number restricted for reasons of personal security or vulnerability; risk assessment for suicide, self-harm or potential threat to counselling staff
Circumstantial:	Family relationships, details of family, parents, partner, children; nature of employment or study
Questionable:	Information here may be recorded but could be seen to be in conflict with the Third Data Protection Principle, which requires that data be 'adequate, relevant and not excessive for their purposes'. Information of questionable relevance (obviously depending upon context), might include sexual orientation, HIV status, history of illicit drug use, etc.

Security and destruction of records

Therapeutic records, by their very nature, often contain sensitive personal information, which may be potentially damaging to the client's interests if in the wrong hands. Therapists and their organisations have a responsibility under data protection law to ensure the security of records, whether computerised or manual in form, via the use of basic security measures, e.g. locked filing cabinets, use of passwords and encryption in computer systems. There is also a responsibility to ensure the safe and confidential destruction of records on their expiry in a way that continues to prevent unauthorised access or use of the records. The responsibility to destroy such records after the death of the therapist is a serious ethical and practical consideration. Therapists are recommended to appoint an executor who will take responsibility for destroying any remaining records in the event of the therapist's death. The responsibility for security of client records is no less onerous for any client records kept at the therapist's home, if working in private practice.

Time limits for retaining counselling and psychotherapy records

The Sixth Data Protection Principle requires that personal data not be held longer than necessary for its purpose. Certain types of record e.g. NHS records, are classed as 'public records', with specified periods for retention. For example, records of patients defined as 'mentally disordered' are kept for 20 years after last treatment, or 8 years after the patient's death. Where no set time limit applies to therapeutic records, therapists and their organisations need to decide an appropriate time limit for keeping records, prior to organising their safe and confidential destruction. Appropriate time limits might reflect the relevant time limits for the use of therapeutic records in responding to a complaint against therapist or agency under BACP procedures (5 years), or the normal time limit for action by the client for negligence (6 years).

4   Summary

Counselling and psychotherapy confidentiality is clearly limited by the powers of discovery held by the legal system, and by the more recent rights of client access under data protection law. Therapists may be influenced by these factors to opt for more objective, minimalist forms of recording which are consistent with the potential inroads of the courts, and comply with data protection principles, but without losing sight of their primary purpose as a record of therapeutic work.

Notes

The term 'therapist' is used to refer to both counsellors and psychotherapists. Therapists need to bear in mind that these guidelines are meant to be accurate and helpful, but that the current rapid pace of change, combined with differences in interpretation, means that there continues to be uncertainty about many of the key issues discussed here. It is always advisable to check and update your own recording practice and that of your agency, with sources such as a professional association, such as BACP, or with your course tutors, if currently on a training course. It is likely that this guidance will itself be updated from time to time.

References

Kellam, A. (1994) 'Police powers to obtain information about patients', Psychiatric Bulletin, 18, 99–100 R. v Cardiff Crown Court, Ex Parte Kellam 7 April 1993.

Peter Jenkins
Senior Lecturer in Counselling Studies
University of Central Lancashire

British Association for
Counselling and Psychotherapy

1 Regent Place
Rugby
Warwickshire CV21 2PJ
Office: 01788 550899
Information Line: 01788 578328
Fax 01788 562189
Minicom: 01788 572838
email: bac@bac.co.uk
http://www.counselling.co.uk
Company limited by guarantee 2175320 • registered in England & Wales • Registered Charity 298361

References

American Psychiatric Association (1980) *Diagnostic and Statistical Manual of Mental Disorders, Third Edition*. Washington, DC: APA.

American Psychiatric Association (1984) *Diagnostic and Statistical Manual of Mental Disorders, Fourth Edition*, Washington, DC: APA.

American Psychiatric Association (1988) 'AIDS policy: confidentiality and disclosure', *American Journal of Psychiatry*, 145: 541–2.

Anderson, H., Goolishian, H. and Winderman, L. (1986) 'Problem determined systems: towards transformation in family therapy', *Journal of Strategic and Systemic Therapies*, 5: 1–14.

Arnett, J. (1999) 'Adolescent storm and stress, reconsidered', *American Psychologist*, 54 (5): 317–26.

Barker, C., Pistrang, N. and Elliot, R. (1994) *Research Methods in Clinical and Counselling Psychology*. Chichester: Wiley.

Barlow, D. and Hersen, M. (1994) *Single Case Experimental Design*. New York: Pergamon.

Barrett, M. and Trevitt, J. (1991) *Attachment Behaviour and the Schoolchild: An Introduction to Educational Therapy*. London: Tavistock.

Beck, A. (1976) *Cognitive Therapy and Emotional Disorders*. New York: International University Press.

Berg, I. and Miller, S. (1992) *Working with the Problem Drinker*. New York: W W Norton.

Birleson, P. (1981) 'The validity of depressive disorder in childhood and the development of a self-rating scale: a research report', *Journal of Child Psychology and Psychiatry*, 22: 73–8.

Birleson, P., Hudson, I. and Buchanan, D. (1987) 'Clinical evaluation of a self-rating scale for depressive disorder in childhood (depression self-rating scale)', *Journal of Child Psychology and Psychiatry*, 28: 43–60.

Black, D. (1993) 'Children and bereavement', *Highlight*, 121. London: National Children's Bureau.

Blake, D.D., Weather, F.W., Nagy, L.M. (1995) 'The development of a clinician administered PTSD scale', *Journal of Traumatic Stress*, 8: 79–80.

Bor, R. and McCann, D. (eds) (1999) *The Practice of Counselling in Primary Care*. London: Sage.

Booth, H., Goodwin, I., Newnes, C. and Dawson, O. (1997) 'Process and outcome of counselling in general practice', *Clinical Psychology Forum*, 101: 32–40.

Brant, S. (1992) 'Hearing the patient's story', *International Journal of Health Care Quality Assurance*, 5: 5–7.

Budman, S. and Gurman, A. (1992) 'A time-sensitive model of brief therapy', in S. Budman, M. Hoyt and S. Friedman (eds), *The First Session in Brief Therapy*. New York: Guildford.

Byng-Hall, J. (1995) *Rewriting Family Scripts*. New York: Guilford Press.

Capewell, E. (1999) *Disseminating the Concept of Crisis Intervention into Education: Mapping the Process*. Paper presented at the 4th International Children and Death Conference, Bristol, September 1999.

Cecchin, G. (1987) 'Hypothesising, circularity, neutrality revisited: an invitation to curiosity', *Family Process*, 26: 405–13.

Chaudhuri, A. (2000) 'Studies in Mortality', *The Times*, 2 February 2000.

Children Act 1989. London: HMSO.

Clarke, N., Elliott, S., Hodgson, C. and Robbins, S. (1994) 'The development of an outcome audit programme for five therapy professions: evaluating the evaluators', *Clinical Psychology Forum*, 70: 26–31.

Copley, B. and Forryan, B. (1997) *Therapeutic Work with Children and Young People*, 2nd edn. London: Cassell.

Cowie, H. and Sharp, S. (1996) *Peer Counselling in Schools: A Time to Listen*. London: David Fulton.

Davis, T. and Osborn, C. (2000) *The Solution-Focused School Counsellor*. Philadelphia: Taylor & Francis.

Daws, D. and Boston, M. (1981) *The Child Psychotherapist and Problems of Young People*. London: Karnac.

DeAngelis, T. (2000a) 'School psychologists: in demand and expanding their reach', *Monitor on Psychology*, pp. 30–1.

DeAngelis, T. (2000b) 'In the aftermath of Columbine', *Monitor on Psychology*, p. 33.

Department of Health (1989) *Working for Patients*. London: HMSO.

Department of Health (1991) *Children Act 1989: Guidance and Regulations*. London: HMSO.

De Shazer, S. (1985) *Keys to Solutions in Brief Therapy*. New York: Norton.

Dohrenwend, B.P., Dohrenwend, B.S., Warkeit, G.J. et al. (1981) 'Stress in the community: a report to the President's commission on the accident at Three Mile Island', *Annals of the New York Academy of Sciences*, 365: 159–74.

Dowling, E. and Osborne, E. (1994) *The Family and the School, Second Edition*. London: Routledge.

Geldard, K. and Geldard, D. (1999a) *Counselling Children: A Practical Introduction*. London: Sage.

Geldard, K. and Geldard, D. (1999b) *Counselling Adolescents*. London: Sage.

Glass, J.C. (1991) 'Death, loss and grief among middle school children: implication for the school counselor', *Elementary School Guidance and Counseling*, 26 (2): 139–48.

Grant, L. and Schakner, H. (1993) 'Coping with the ultimate tragedy – the death of a student', *NAASP Bulletin*, April 1993: 1–9.

Griffiths, R. (1983) *NHS Management Enquiry (The Griffiths Report)*. London: HMSO.

Halstead, J. (1996) 'Psychotherapy outcome audit: what is not going on?', *Clinical Psychology Journal*, 90: 5–7.

Hamblin, D. (1974) *The Teacher and Counselling*. Oxford: Blackwell.

Harris-Hendriks, J., Black, D. and Kaplan, T. (1993) *When Father Kills Mother: Guiding Children Through Trauma and Grief*. London: Routledge.

Harris-Hendriks, J. and Newman, M. (1995) 'Psychological trauma in children and adolescents', *Advances in Psychiatric Treatment*, 1: 170–5.

Hawton, K., Salkovskis, P., Kirk, J. and Clark, D. (1994) *Cognitive Behaviour Therapy for Psychiatric Problems: A Practical Guide*. Oxford: Oxford University Press.

Hewson, S. (1994) 'Clinicians' role in measuring outcomes', *Clinical Psychology Forum*, 74: 31–2.

Hockey, J., Katz, J. and Small, N. (2001) *Grief Mourning and Death Ritual*. Philadelphia, PA: Open University.

Hodgkinson, P.E. and Stewart, M. (eds) (1991) *Coping with Catastrophe – A Handbook of Disaster Management*. London: Routledge.

Horowitz, M.J., Wilner, N. and Alvarez, W. (1979) 'Impact of events scale: a measure of subjective distress', *Psychosomatic Medicine*, 41: 209–18.

Jackson, R. and Juniper, D.F. (1971) *A Manual of Education Guidance*. London: Holt, Rinehart and Winston.

Jones, D. (1992) *Liverpool response to Hillsborough disaster*. Lecture, Liverpool Education Centre.

Jones, A. (1970) *School Counselling in Practice*. London: Ward Lock Educational.

Karpel, M. (1980) 'Family secrets', *Family Process*, 19: 295–306.

Kastenbaum, R. (1977) 'Death and development through the life span', in H. Fiefel (ed.), *New Meanings of Death*. New York: McGraw-Hill. pp. 17–45.

Kiresuk, T.J. and Choate, R.O. (1994) 'Applications of goal attainment scaling', in T.J. Kiresuk, A. Smith and J.E. Cardillo (eds), *Goal Attainment Scaling: Applications, Theory and Measurement*. Hillsdale, NJ: Lawrence Erlbaum.

Kubler-Ross, E. (1983) *On Children and Death*. New York: Macmillan.

Lansdown, R. and Benjamin, G. (1985) 'The development of the concept of death in children aged 5-9 years', *Child: Care, Health and Development*, 11: 13–20.

Lanyado, M. and Horne, A. (1999) *The Handbook of Child and Adolescent Psychotherapy*. London: Routledge.

Leaman, O. (1995) *Death and Loss: Compassionate Approaches in the Classroom*. London: Cassell Studies in Pastoral Care and Personal and Social Education.

McDaniel, S., Hepworth, J. and Doherty, W. (1992) *Medical Family Therapy*. New York: Basic Books.

McFarlane, A.C. (1987) 'Post-traumatic phenomena in a longitudinal study of children following a natural disaster', *Journal of the American Academy of Child and Adolescent Pyschiatry*, 26: 764–9.

McGoldrick, M. and Gerson, R. (1985) *Genograms in Family Assessment*. New York: Norton.

McLeod, J. (1994) *Doing Counselling Research*. London: Sage.

Martin, D. (1989) *Counselling and Therapy Skills*. Illinois: Waveland Press.

Miller, S., Duncan, B. and Hubble, M. (1997) *Escape from Babel*. New York: Norton.

Milner, P. (1974) *Counselling in Education*. London, Dent.

Mitchell, J.I. (1983) 'When disaster strikes … the critical incident debriefing process', *Journal of the Emergency Services*, 8: 36–9.

Neilson, J. (1994) 'Therapist–patient concordance on therapy process and outcome and its implications for service evaluation', *Clinical Psychology Forum*, 73: 5–7.

Newcombe, N. (1996) *Child Development*. London: HarperCollins.

O'Hara, D.M., Taylor, R. and Simpson, K. (1994) 'Critical incident stress debriefing support in school – developing a role for an LEA Psychology Service', *Educational Psychology in Practice*, 10 (1): 27–33.

Palazzoli, S., Boscolo, C., Cecchin, G. and Prata, G. (1980a) 'The problem of the referring person', *Journal of Marital and Family Therapy*, 6: 3–9.

Palazzoli, S., Prata, G., Boscolo, C. and Cecchin, G. (1980b) 'Hypothesizing, circularity, neutrality. Three guidelines for the conductor of the session', *Family Process*, 19: 3–12.

Parker, J., Watts, H. and Allsopp, M.R. (1995) 'Post-traumatic stress symptoms in children and parents following a school-based fatality', *Childcare, Health and Development*, 21 (3): 183–9.

Pynoos, R.S., Frederick, C., Nader, K., Arroyo, W., Steinberg, A., Eth, S., Nunez, F. and Fairbanks, L. (1987) 'Life threat and post-traumatic stress in school-age children', *Archives of General Psychiatry*, 44: 1057–63.

Reynolds, C.R. and Richmond, B.D. (1978) 'What I think and feel: a revised measure of children's manifest anxiety', *Journal of Abnormal Child Psychology*, 6: 271–80.

Rogers, C. (1951) *Client-Centered Therapy*. Boston: Houghton Mifflin.

Rogers, C. (1961) *On Becoming a Person*. Boston: Houghton Mifflin.

Sorensen, J. (1989) 'Responding to student or teacher death: preplanning crisis intervention', *Journal of Counseling and Development*, 21 (3): 183–9.

Speece, M.W. and Brent, S.B. (1984) 'Children's understanding of death: a review of three components of a death concept', *Child Development*, 55: 1671–89.

Stevenson, R.G. and Stevenson, E.P. (1996) 'Adolescents and education about death, dying and bereavement', in C.A. Corr and D.E. Balk (eds), *Handbook of Adolescent Death and Bereavement*. Springer: New York.

Stiles, W.B. (1980) 'Measurement of the impact of psychotherapy session', *Journal of Consulting and Clinical Psychology*, 48 (2): 176–85.

Stroebe, M.S. and Schut, H. (1995) 'Grief', in A. Manstead and M. Hughstone (eds), *Blackwell Dictionary of Social Psychology*. Oxford: Blackwell.

Strong, T. (2000) 'Six orienting ideas for collaborative counsellors', *European Journal of Psychotherapy, Counselling and Health*, 3 (1): 25–42.

Tolley, K. and Rowlands, N. (1995) *Evaluating the Cost-Effectiveness of Counselling in Health Care*. London: Routledge.

Tomm, K. (1987) 'Interventive interviewing, Part 1: Strategizing as a fourth guideline for the therapist', *Family Process*, 23: 3–13.

Udwin, A. (1993) 'Annotation: children's reactions to traumatic events', *Journal of Child Psychology and Psychiatry*, 34: 115–27.

Van Der Kolk, B.A., Dreyfuss, D., Michaels, M., Shera, D., Berkowitz, R. and Fisler, R. (1994) 'Fluoxetine in post traumatic stress disorder', *Journal of Child Psychiatry*, 55: 517–22.

Weiss, D. (1997) 'Structured clinical interview techniques', in J.P. Wilson and T.M. Keane (eds), *Assessing Psychological Trauma and PTSD*. New York: Guildford Press.

World Health Organisation (1992) *United Nations Programme of Humanitarian Assistance in Yugoslavia: WHO Mission on the Mental Health Needs of Refugees, Displaced Persons and Others Affected by the Conflict*. Geneva: WHO.

Wright, L., Watson, W. and Bell, J. (1996) *Beliefs: The Heart of Healing in Families and Illness*. New York: Basic Books.

Yule, W. and Gold, A. (1993) *Wise Before the Event: Coping with Crises in Schools*. Portugal: Calouste Gulbenkian Foundation.

Yule, W. and Udwin, O. (1991) 'Screening child survivors for post-traumatic stress disorders: experiences from the "Jupiter" sinking', *British Journal of Clinical Psychology*, 30: 131–8.

Index